# Great American Writers
## TWENTIETH CENTURY

EDITOR
### R. BAIRD SHUMAN
*University of Illinois*

Ernest Gaines • John Gardner

William Gibson • Nikki Giovanni • Lorraine Hansberry

Ernest Hemingway • John Hersey • S. E. Hinton

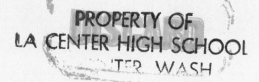

MARSHALL CAVENDISH
NEW YORK • TORONTO • LONDON • SYDNEY

Marshall Cavendish
99 White Plains Road
Tarrytown, New York 10591-9001

Website: www.marshallcavendish.com

© 2002 Marshall Cavendish Corporation

**Salem Press**

     Editor: R. Baird Shuman
     Managing Editor: R. Kent Rasmussen

     Manuscript Editors: Heather Stratton
                     Lauren M. Mitchell
     Assistant Editor: Andrea Miller
     Research Supervisor: Jeffry Jensen
     Acquisitions Editor: Mark Rehn

**Marshall Cavendish**

     Project Editor: Marian Armstrong
     Editorial Director: Paul Bernabeo

Designer: Patrice Sheridan

Photo Research: Candlepants
                 Carousel Research
                 Linda Sykes Picture Research
                 Anne Burns Images

Indexing: AEIOU

**Library of Congress Cataloging-in-Publication Data**

Great American writers: twentieth century / R. Baird Shuman, editor.
    v. cm.
    Includes bibliographical references and indexes.
    Contents: v. 5. Agee-Bellow--v. 2. Benét-Cather--v. 3. Cormier-
Dylan--v. 4. Eliot-Frost--v. 5. Gaines-Hinton--v. 6. Hughes-Lewis--v. 7.
London-McNickle--v. 8. Miller-O'Connor--v. 9. O'Neill-Rich--v. 10.
Salinger-Stein--v. 11. Steinbeck-Walker--v. 12. Welty-Zindel--v. 13.
Index.
    ISBN 0-7614-7240-1 (set)—ISBN 0-7614-7245-2 (v. 5)
    1. American literature--20th century--Bio-bibliography--
Dictionaries. 2. Authors, American--20th century--Biography--
Dictionaries. 3. American literature--20th century--Dictionaries. I.
Shuman, R. Baird (Robert Baird), 1929-

PS221.G74 2002
810.9'005'03
[B]                                   2001028461

Printed in Malaysia; bound in the United States

07 06 05 04    6 5 4 3 2

**Volume 5 Illustration Credits**
(a = above, b = below, l = left, r = right)

Anthony Potter Collection/Archive Photos: 664
AP/Wide World: cover portrait of William Gibson, 612
Archive Photos: 611, 661 (t)
Arte & Immagini/Corbis: 614 (l)
Courtesy the Artist: 704, 715
Bantam Doubleday Dell: 706
Bettmann/Corbis: cover portrait of Lorraine Hansberry, 620, 625, 629,
637, 645, 647, 648, 651, 656, 669 (l & r), 697
Blanchard-Hill Collection/Courtesy American Primitive Gallery, NY: 600
Corbis: 614 (right), 688
Culver Pictures: cover portrait of John Hersey, 591, 617, 648, 660,
683, 684, 707, 709
Eli Broad Family Foundation, Santa Monica, California. Courtesy Curt
Marcus Gallery, NY: 675
Michael Evans/NYT/Archive Photos: cover portrait of Nikki Giovanni, 627
The Everett Collection: 700
Courtesy Fay Gold Gallery, Atlanta: 632
Fotos International/Archive Photos: 701
Fukushima Prefectural Museum of Art, Japan/VAGA, NY: 695
© Joel Gardner: cover portrait of John Gardner, 596
Courtesy George Adams Gallery, NY. Sydney and Walda Besthoff
Foundation: 608
Phillip Gould/Corbis: cover portrait of Ernest Gaines, 581, 582, 586,
588
Ken Heyman/Woodfin Camp: cover portrait of Ernest Hemingway, 659
Courtesy Jan Baum Gallery, Los Angeles, California: 624, 655, 705
John F. Kennedy Library: 662, 667
Clemens Kalischer: 613
Courtesy the Artist/Collection Krannert Art Museum, University of
Illinois, Champaign: 693
Laurie Platt Winfrey, Inc.: 597, 665
Library of Congress: 694
Meyer Liebowitz/NYT/Archive Photos: 630
Courtesy Louis K. Meisel Gallery, NY: 606
Courtesy Whitfield Lovell and DC Moore Gallery, NY: 657
Detail #1, Courtesy Whitfield Lovell and DC Moore Gallery, NY,
photo by Steve Dennie: 587
Courtesy of the artist, Regina McFadden: 666
Montgomery Museum of Fine Arts. © VAGA, NY: 685
Larry Morris/NYT/Archive Photos: 630 (l)
National Academy of Design, NY, Estate of Charles White and
Heritage Gallery: 628
Courtesy Penguin Putnam, Inc.: cover portrait of S. E. Hinton, 699
From *That Was Then, This Is Now* by S. E. Hinton, cover illustration
by Robert Hunt, copyright © 1998 by Robert Hunt, cover illustration
Used by permission of Puffin Books, an imprint of Penguin Putnam
Books for Young Readers, a division of Penguin Putnam, Inc.: 703
Philadelphia Museum of Art, Gift of Dr. and Mrs. Matthew T. Moore: 641
Photofest: 590, 592, 618, 621, 672, 673, 677, 681, 691, 708, 717
Courtesy Portal Gallery, London: 623
Courtesy P.P.O.W. Gallery, NY: 712
Private Collection: 661 (b), 662 (inset), 663
© Jan B. Quackenbush: 595
Réunion des Musées Nationaux/Art Resource, NY/© ARS, NY: 680
Courtesy the Artist and Ronald Feldman Fine Arts, NY: 686
© Betye Saar, Courtesy Michael Rosenfeld Gallery, NY: 638, 644
The Saint Louis Art Museum. ©VAGA, NY: 689
Simon & Schuster Inc.: 674
Smithsonian American Art Museum/Art Resource, NY: 583, 605, 646,
650, 653
Smithsonian American Art Museum/Art Resource, NY. © VAGA, NY: 603
Courtesy the Artist/Stone: 714
Studio Museum in Harlem, gift of Stuart Liebman in memory of
Joseph Liebman: 643
Courtesy Tatistcheff & Co., NY: 609
Private Collection, Courtesy Terry Distenfass Gallery, NY. © VAGA,
NY: 640
Reprinted by permission of Vintage Books and Ballantine Books,
Divisions of Random House, Inc.: 585, 589, 599, 649, 654, 687, 690
Warner Brothers/Archive Photos: 711
William Morrow and Company, Inc.: 631
Todd Wright/Courtesy the author: 633

# Contents

# Ernest J. Gaines

**BORN:** January 15, 1933, Oscar, Louisiana
**IDENTIFICATION:** Contemporary African American writer, best known
for novels of rural black life in the southern United States.

Ernest J. Gaines's realistic stories are deeply rooted in the southern black culture that had been largely ignored for years in American literature. Gaines in-
terweaves African American folk traditions with the rich dialects that were
spoken by the poor black and white farmers on southern plantations. Gaines's
themes are universal, including those of social and racial conflict, men's relationships with their fathers, and the power and importance of dignity. Gaines
has been criticized for being insufficiently political in his protest of American
racism, but he said that it is most important to him to write about what he
knows well, creating convincing characters in interesting and enjoyable stories that appeal to people of all races.

# The Writer's Life

Ernest James Gaines was born on January 15, 1933, on the River Lake Plantation near Oscar, Louisiana. He was the oldest of five children of Manuel and Adrienne Colar Gaines, tenant farmers. Gaines spent his childhood on the plantation and was profoundly influenced by many of his experiences there. He fished in the swamps with the old people, hearing their tales and ghost stories. He observed the differences between the black and white cultures of the plantation and the nearby town.

**Southern Childhood.** By the time he was nine years old, Gaines was working in the fields for fifty cents a day. While his parents worked, Gaines and his younger brothers and sisters were cared for by their aunt, Miss Augusteen Jefferson, who was unable to walk but nonetheless was strong and dignified. She crawled from the house to the garden and cooked and cleaned, never allowing her inability to walk to keep her from disciplining and providing for the children. Because Miss Augusteen could not travel, people gathered at her house to socialize. There was no radio or television, so visitors spent time talking, telling stories about local events, past and present. His visiting neighbors gave Gaines a lifelong sense of community and constant opportunities to hear stories. From these stories he absorbed the smells, tastes, and sounds of Louisiana and began to become an extraordinary storyteller himself.

Photographer Philip Gould snapped this photograph of Gaines in Lafayette, Louisiana, in 1984, the year Gaines joined the University of Southwestern Louisiana in Lafayette as a professor of creative writing.

William H. Johnson's *Folk Family* (The Smithsonian American Art Museum, Washington, D.C.), ca. 1940, captures the rural folk setting that sowed the seeds to what would one day become a flourishing writing career for Gaines.

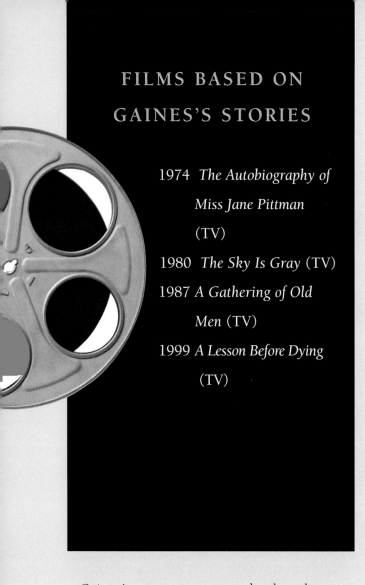

Gaines's parents separated when he was eight years old, and his mother moved to Vallejo in northern California. Gaines remained in Louisiana, living with Miss Augusteen and helping her take care of the younger children. When his father left Louisiana, Gaines lost contact with him. Gaines has said that he never quite recovered from his father's absence. The absent father and damaged father-son relationship would become a powerful theme throughout his fiction.

**The Young Writer.** Gaines moved to California at fifteen to join his mother and her new husband and his seven children. Discouraged by his stepfather from associating with the idle teenagers in town and homesick for Louisiana, Gaines began reading extensively. He read the works of authors who wrote about rural people and peasant life, such as the modern American writers William Faulkner and Ernest Hemingway, as well as the nineteenth-century Russian novelists Ivan Turgenev and Leo Tolstoy.

Gaines realized that the kinds of people he had known growing up in Louisiana were absent from the stories he read, and he was inspired to write about them. In his midteens he began his first novel, *A Little Stream,* in which he tried to create a true portrait of Louisiana bayou life. It was rejected by publishers, but he was not discouraged. He became more determined than ever to become a successful writer.

After high school, Gaines attended Vallejo Junior College, and he served in the army from 1953 to 1955. Gaines enrolled at San Francisco State College as an English major in 1955, also working as a postal clerk and an apprentice printer. In 1956 his short story "The Turtles" appeared in the small San Francisco magazine *Transfer*, providing his first literary success. This story caught the attention of an independent literary agent named Dorothea Oppenheimer, who urged Gaines to send her anything he wrote. Until her death in 1987, Oppenheimer was an important source of emotional support and friendship for Gaines.

During 1958 and 1959 Gaines studied creative writing at Stanford University with the assistance of a Wallace Stegner Fellowship in creative writing. There he read a wide range of authors and began what would become his signature stories about the folk culture of rural Louisiana. In 1959 Gaines won the Joseph Henry Jackson Award for the story "Comeback" and resumed work on "A Little Stream," the novel he had begun as a teenager. Gaines soon realized that if he were to write truthfully about the life he had known in Louisiana, he must return there, and he did so, for six months. In the South once again, Gaines completed the work that in 1964 became *Catherine Carmier,* his first published novel.

**Mastering the Writer's Craft.** *Catherine Carmier* was hardly noticed by literary critics and earned Gaines no money. However, Gaines

# HIGHLIGHTS IN GAINES'S LIFE

| | |
|---|---|
| **1933** | Ernest James Gaines is born on January 15 at River Lake Plantation near Oscar, Louisiana. |
| **1933–1941** | Lives with family including his aunt, Augusteen Jefferson. |
| **1941** | Parents separate; with siblings remains in Louisiana with his aunt; loses contact with his father. |
| **1948** | Moves to California to join his mother, her new husband, and her husband's children. |
| **1953–1955** | Serves in the U.S. Army. |
| **1955–1957** | Attends Vallejo Junior College and San Francisco State College. |
| **1956** | Publishes first stories in San Francisco magazine *Transfer*. |
| **1958–1959** | Studies creative writing at Stanford University. |
| **1959** | Receives Joseph Henry Jackson Award for short story "Comeback." |
| **1964** | Publishes first novel, *Catherine Carmier*. |
| **1967** | Publishes second novel, *Of Love and Dust*; receives National Endowment for the Arts grant. |
| **1968** | Publishes *Bloodline*, a collection of short stories. |
| **1971** | Publishes *The Autobiography of Miss Jane Pittman*, a novel. |
| **1972** | Receives Gold Medal Award for *The Autobiography of Miss Jane Pittman*. |
| **1974** | Television adaptation of *The Autobiography of Miss Jane Pittman* wins nine Emmy Awards. |
| **1978** | Publishes third novel, *In My Father's House*. |
| **1980** | Receives honorary doctorate of letters from Denison University. |
| **1981** | Writer-in-residence at Stanford University. |
| **1983** | Publishes *A Gathering of Old Men*; is writer-in-residence at University of Southwestern Louisiana. |
| **1984** | Begins teaching creative writing at University of Southwestern Louisiana; receives Gold Medal Award for *A Gathering of Old Men*. |
| **1986** | Writer-in-residence at Whittier College, from which he receives honorary doctorate of letters. |
| **1987** | Receives honorary doctorate of letters from Louisiana State University. |
| **1993** | Publishes *A Lesson Before Dying*; receives Genius Award from the MacArthur Foundation; marries Dianne Saulney. |
| **1994** | Receives National Book Critics Circle Award for *A Lesson Before Dying*. |

Gaines revisits his roots as he walks along a dirt road near the River Lake Plantation, the place of his birth, in 1995. The people of this region—his beloved aunt, his siblings, his neighbors—had a profound impact on his writing career. He spent his childhood drinking in their stories, until he, too, could weave a tale with the best of them.

was determined to establish his reputation and continued to be a disciplined writer, writing "five hours a day, five days a week." In 1967 his second novel, *Of Love and Dust*, was published. *Bloodline*, a collection of five short stories, followed in 1968. These two works earned Gaines a positive reputation; in the early 1970s he received several prestigious literary awards and became writer-in-residence at Denison University in Granville, Ohio. Gaines's reputation as a master storyteller was further enhanced by the publication in 1971 of *The Autobiography of Miss Jane Pittman*, now considered his classic masterpiece. The novel's successful 1974 television adaptation won nine Emmy Awards and brought Gaines much hardwon national attention.

Gaines's next novel, *In My Father's House*, was published in 1978. It received mixed reviews, and Gaines himself was not entirely satisfied with this work. Gaines spent 1981 as writer-in-residence at Stanford University, where he began work on *A Gathering of Old Men*, published in 1983. His reputation was strengthened in the 1980s by television adaptations of his short story "The Sky Is Gray" and *A Gathering of Old Men*. In 1984 Gaines was made professor of creative writing at the University of Southwestern Louisiana in Lafayette.

With the successful publication in 1993 of *A Lesson Before Dying*, Gaines secured his status as one of America's most honest and important contemporary chroniclers of rural black life. In 1993 Gaines won a prestigious Genius Award from the MacArthur Foundation and was married to Dianne Saulney. *A Lesson Before Dying* was adapted for television in 1999.

Ernest J. Gaines writes about the struggle of the rural American underclass to live with dignity; to find love, family, and community; and to know what it means to be human. His stories take place in a part of the country where unofficial segregation determines many choices in life. Gaines is admired for his compassionate portrayal of ordinary people whose most heroic qualities are strength of character and unshakable dignity in humiliating and dehumanizing circumstances. He is considered highly skilled in his use of first-person narration, learned from the traditions of African American folk storytelling and modeled on the novels of fellow southern writer William Faulkner.

Gaines, like Faulkner, has been praised for his ability to effectively reflect human experience in the small world of a single story. Gaines's characters are fictional, but many are modeled on real people he knew as a young boy in rural Louisiana. He writes with humor and compassion about the places and people he knew. Gaines is best known for his novels, which are important records of a world that had been largely ignored in previous American literature. Some early short stories were published as a collection, and *A Long Day in November* (1971) was also published separately. His story "The Sky Is Gray" was adapted for television in 1980.

**Varied Southern Cultures.** The term *Creole* describes both white Europeans born in the West Indies and their descendants, as well as people of mixed black and white races. Most plantation owners in Gaines's stories have French names,

because they are descendants of the French who settled in many parts of North America. The Acadian French immigrants who settled specifically in Newfoundland and Nova Scotia and later migrated to Louisiana are called Cajuns (from "Acadian"). They are white but occupy a lower socioeconomic class than the white plantation bosses, also often of French

A blend of storytelling and still photography, artist Whitfield Lovell's 1999 installation of a one-room house, *Whispers from the Walls*, echoes Gaines's extraordinary ability to bring the past to life. The voices of the people Gaines knew as a boy growing up, the poor southern farmers of Louisiana, are amplified in Gaines's proficient and authentic use of southern dialect.

extraction. The Cajuns were favored by the other white landowners and were able to take the best farmland, displacing black and Creole farmers, who felt unable to protest. The anger and self-hatred of Gaines's characters in the face of this humiliating exploitation is particularly poignant. His characters' social classes parallel those of William Faulkner's South, with the dying aristocracy of "old money" looking down on a permanent economic and social underclass.

**The Authentic Voice of a People.** *Catherine Carmier*, which examines love and

## SOME INSPIRATIONS BEHIND GAINES'S WORK

Gaines said that his aunt, Miss Augusteen Jefferson, taught him how to live with dignity. She is the model for the strong women in his fiction, who refuse to allow themselves or the people they love to be defeated by misfortune. An aunt or godmother figure like Miss Augusteen is often important in Gaines's stories; the spirit of Miss Jane in *The Autobiography of Miss Jane Pittman* is a good example.

Gaines realized that there were no characters in stories he read like the black and Creole people he had known as a young boy in Louisiana, so he invented his own characters to speak with the rhythms and dialect of southern African American speech. He listened to old people tell stories at his aunt's house and went fishing with them in the swamps. His characters, such as the group in *A Gathering of Old Men*, embody the difficulties of aging as well as the power gained by finally standing up against a life of abuse.

The absence of Gaines's father clearly affected him. In both *A Lesson Before Dying* and *In My Father's House*, the central themes are the separation of fathers and sons and the struggle to attain or regain manhood. Gaines's work is also frequently concerned with the ways in which African American families have been devastated through slavery, economic hardship, racism, and other social pressures.

Gaines read widely when he was young and especially loved stories about rural peasant life. The nineteenth-century Russian writer Ivan Turgenev's *Fathers and Sons* (1867) was the outline for Gaines's first novel, *Catherine Carmier*. The influence of the American writer William Faulkner is felt in several ways: in Gaines's use of authentic southern dialects; in his use of a fictional southern town, Bayonne, Louisiana; and in his use of multiple first-person narration, in which each character tells his or her own story.

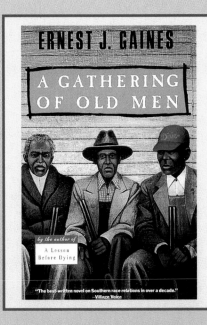

## LONG FICTION

1964    Catherine Carmier
1967    Of Love and Dust
1971    The Autobiography of
        Miss Jane Pittman
1978    In My Father's House
1983    A Gathering of Old Men
1993    A Lesson Before Dying

## SHORT FICTION

1968    Bloodline
1971    A Long Day in
        November

racial prejudice, received no praise from reviewers but was considered evidence of Gaines's potential. *Of Love and Dust*, another dramatic story of racial tension, forbidden romance, and self-discovery, was more popular and brought Gaines enough money to support himself as a full-time writer. His next book, *Bloodline*, a collection of five short stories also received good reviews. However, Gaines is most celebrated for his important 1971 novel, *The Autobiography of Miss Jane Pittman*, which is considered his masterpiece. The novel was successfully adapted for television in 1974. *In My Father's House* (1978) received some positive reviews and strengthened Gaines's reputation, but Gaines himself was displeased with it.

In 1981 Gaines became writer-in-residence at Stanford University in California, where he began work on *A Gathering of Old Men* (1983), a powerful story about racial conflict and the devastation of hatred. His next work, *A Lesson Before Dying* appeared ten years later. It also was filmed for television.

Gaines has been admired less for his stories' plots than for his characters and the voices in which they tell their histories. His portrayals of black families—particularly sons and fathers—separated by cruelty and misfortune are unusually poignant and authentic. White and black narrators present multiple first-person points of view. Gaines's skillful use of dialect shows his perfect ear for the rhythms of regional speech.

## BIBLIOGRAPHY

Babb, Valerie-Melissa. *Ernest Gaines*. Boston: Twayne Publishers, 1991.

Barrow, Craig W. "Ernest J. Gaines: Overview." In *Twentieth-Century Young Adult Writers*. Detroit: St. James Press, 1994.

Carmeau, Karen. *Ernest J. Gaines: A Critical Companion*. Westport, Conn.: Greenwood Press, 1998.

Doyle, Mary Ellen. "Ernest J. Gaines: An Annotated Bibliography, 1956–1988." *Black American Literature Forum* 24 (Spring, 1990): 125–150.

Estes, David, ed. *Critical Reflections on the Fiction of Ernest J. Gaines*. Athens: University of Georgia Press, 1994.

Gaudet, Marcia, and Carl Wooton. *Porch Talk with Ernest Gaines: Conversations on the Writer's Craft*. Baton Rouge: Louisiana State University Press, 1990.

Gayle, Addison, Jr. *The Way of the New World: The Black Novel in America*. New York: Doubleday, 1975.

Hudson, Theodore R. *The History of Southern Literature*. Baton Rouge: Louisiana State University Press, 1985.

Peden, William. *The American Short Story: Continuity and Change, 1940–1975*. Boston: Houghton Mifflin, 1975.

Simpson, Anne K. *A Gathering of Gaines: The Man and the Writer*. Lafayette: University of Southwestern Louisiana Press, 1991.

# Reader's Guide to Major Works

## THE AUTOBIOGRAPHY OF MISS JANE PITTMAN

**Genre:** Novel
**Subgenre:** Fictional autobiography
**Published:** New York, 1971
**Time period:** From the 1860s to the 1960s
**Setting:** Southern United States

**Themes and Issues.** Miss Jane Pittman represents the enduring strength of the human spirit. She narrates her life, which parallels the history of African Americans from the Civil War in the 1860s to the great accomplishments of the Civil Rights movement of the 1960s that ended segregation of blacks and whites. As a young girl Miss Jane lives in the South; she is an orphaned slave and is beaten for disobeying. When the Civil War is over, she believes that African Americans will find freedom and opportunity in the North. She and others also come to believe in "the One," a black leader who will set African Americans free from their long bondage. She eventually learns and inspires others that "freedom is not a place" and risks everything to gain her self-respect and dignity, which finally set her free.

**The Plot.** A young teacher interviews Miss Jane, who is more than one hundred years old. Miss Jane recalls many significant moments in southern history. As a young girl, she is called by a slave name, Ticey. At twelve, the young girl impresses a Northern soldier, Corporal Brown, who is passing through the plantation. He gives her a new name, Jane Brown, after his own daughter. This sign of respect inspires great hope in the young girl. She refuses to be subservient and no longer answers to her slave name.

Jane convinces a group of slaves to leave the plantation when the war is over and head north to seek freedom and opportunity. They become lost, and only Jane and the young boy Ned survive; Jane takes care of Ned as if he

Actress Cicely Tyson, who portrays Miss Jane Pittman, sips from the "whites only" water fountain in this still from the 1974 Emmy Award–winning television adaptation of Gaines's 1971 masterpiece novel, *The Autobiography of Miss Jane Pittman*.

were her own son. They keep traveling but are soon exhausted and settle on a plantation. Jane, who has never learned to read or write, works and pays for Ned to go to school. When Ned is grown and has moved to Kansas, Jane marries Joe Pittman, and they work on a ranch until Joe, whom Jane loves very much, is killed by a wild stallion. Ned returns to the South hoping to make life better for African Americans there, but he is murdered by racists.

Miss Jane and her community come to believe that a young boy in their town, Jimmy Aaron, is "the One," the savior they long for. In another tragic act of violence, Jimmy is also murdered by racists. Miss Jane's long life of grief and anger gives her the strength to finally commit a simple but powerful act of civil disobedience. On the morning Jimmy is murdered, she walks past a crowd and drinks from the "whites only" water fountain. By this simple act, she declares herself free and helps set the stage for the coming civil rights struggle.

**Analysis.** Miss Jane's autobiographical record and she herself were invented by Gaines, who successfully convinces the reader that the conversations that make up the book are actually taped interviews. Miss Jane is like Rosa Parks, whose simple, courageous act of refusing to give up her seat on a bus to a white person sparked the Civil Rights movement. Miss Jane's self-respect and faith inspire her to take big risks in small actions, revealing that it is each person's individual responsibility to help make a better life for all people.

### SOURCES FOR FURTHER STUDY

"The Autobiography of Miss Jane Pittman, by Ernest J. Gaines." In *Novels for Students: Presenting Analysis, Context, and Criticism on Commonly Studied Novels*, edited by Sheryl Ciccarelli and Marie Rose Napierkowski. Vol. 5. Detroit: Gale Research, 1999.

Charney, Mark J. "Voice and Perspective in the Film Adaptations of Gaines's Fiction." In *Critical Reflections on the Fiction of Ernest J. Gaines*, edited by David C. Estes. Athens: University of Georgia Press, 1994.

Cooper, William J., and Thomas E. Terrill. *The American South: A History*. New York: Knopf, 1990.

## A GATHERING OF OLD MEN

**Genre:** Novel
**Subgenre:** Psychological realism
**Published:** New York, 1983
**Time period:** 1980s
**Setting:** Louisiana plantation

**Themes and Issues.** The collision of long-held traditions with inevitable social change in the new South is a frequent and powerful theme in Ernest J. Gaines's work. *A Gathering of Old Men* is an allegory of the slow passing of these traditions, expressed in the rich dialect and authentic rhythms of southern speech. The novel explores social and racial prejudices against African Americans. The elderly men at the center of the story have been exploited and treated unfairly all their lives. Their families have been intimidated, and their opportunities to farm good land have been taken by the Cajuns and other whites. Powerless to defend themselves,

The life of Charles Mitchell (above), a southern World War II veteran photographed for a 1946 news story, mirrors the lives and exploitation of the men in Gaines's 1983 novel, *A Gathering of Old Men*. Like the men in Gaines's story, Mitchell has been forced to make the most of the only land he could get, in his case the ruins of a mine hole.

their land, and their families, they have suppressed years of anger and frustration. They have been deprived of their dignity and their manhood. The men whose voices are heard in this novel put a symbolic end to what is left of the old way of life in the American South.

**The Plot.** The story is told from the points of view of more than seventeen characters, black, white, and Cajun. The action takes place on a sugarcane plantation owned by Marshall and his daughter, Candy, who are white. When Beau Boutan, a member of a violent and racist Cajun family, is murdered, seventeen old African American men and Candy all confess to the crime. The sheriff is mystified to find that each of the men has with him a recently fired shotgun, as does Candy. The family of the dead man plans to lynch whichever black man they decide has committed the murder. The old men gather around the body and each one describes his motives for committing such a crime. Many of the men have daughters who have been raped and sons who have been unjustly jailed. All of them have been humiliated, subjugated, and exploited by the landowners and deprived of their manhood by the white community.

**Analysis.** After the Civil War and the abolition of slavery, rigid social codes kept black, white, Cajun, and Creole people separate and hostile toward one another. Although Beau Boutan has not personally caused all of the men's suffering, he represents the white community's hostility toward black people, especially black men. The single event of the murder at the center of the novel allows each man to tell a similar story of subjugation and humiliation. Beau Boutan represents Louisiana's class and racial rules, and his murder represents a defiant and liberating act against these rules that propagate self-hatred and shame.

### SOURCES FOR FURTHER STUDY

Dominguez, Virginia R. *White by Definition: Social Classification in Creole Louisiana.* Reprint. New Brunswick, N.J.: Rutgers University Press, 1986.

Harper, Mary T. "From Sons to Fathers: Ernest Gaines's

*A Gathering of Old Men.*" College Language Association Journal 31 (1988): 299–308.

Kenney, W. P. "*A Gathering of Old Men,* by Ernest J. Gaines." In *Masterplots II: African American Fiction Series,* edited by Frank N. Magill. Vol. 1. Pasadena, Calif.: Salem Press, 1994.

## A LESSON BEFORE DYING
**Genre:** Novel
**Subgenre:** Social realism
**Published:** New York, 1993
**Time period:** 1948
**Setting:** Louisiana plantation and fictional town

**Themes and Issues.** Jefferson, wrongly accused of a crime and waiting to be executed, can be seen as the sacrifice of a helpless, uneducated man for the crimes of others. The state's responsibility to free an innocent person is denied because of the long-standing hatred between blacks and whites. Racial tension and

Actress Irma P. Hall, who plays Miss Glenn, and actor Mekhi Phifer, who plays Jefferson, embrace in the 1999 Home Box Office adaptation of Gaines's *A Lesson Before Dying,* the story of an innocent black man sentenced to death by a jury of twelve white men in the South.

failure have made Jefferson hate himself; regaining his manhood through self-respect allows him to die with dignity and in the process also transforms an educated schoolteacher.

**The Plot.** Jefferson is a naïve, barely literate young black man who works in the plantation cane fields. He innocently befriends two men who rob a liquor store and are killed along with the proprietor. Jefferson is innocent but is implicated by his presence at the scene. A jury of twelve white men sentences him to death. Jefferson's defense attorney tries to save him by saying he is just a dumb animal, incapable of committing a crime. Jefferson's godmother, Miss Glenn, determines that he will not be degraded and will go to his death as a man, with dignity.

Another young black man, Grant Wiggins, grew up in Bayonne but left to go to college. He has returned to Bayonne to teach, but he despairs about the bleak futures of his young students and is unsure whether his teaching makes any difference in their lives. Miss Glenn and Grant's aunt, Tante Lou, are friends. The two women ask Grant to visit Jefferson in jail and help him understand that he is a worthy human being and not subhuman, as his lawyer suggests. Grant hesitates but finally agrees to visit Jefferson. Slowly, through Grant's friendship, Jefferson comes to see himself as a person of worth. He dies, but as his aunt and community had hoped, with dignity, knowing that he was valued.

**Analysis.** A tragedy of injustice, *A Lesson Before Dying* is about the commitment to something outside of oneself and the transformative power of pride and self-respect. Jefferson is doomed by class and racial bias. Grant feels despair about his students' futures and does not believe that his education and values can make a difference in their lives. Through an act of kindness encouraged by wise and caring older women, both of the novel's central male characters are transformed. They find dignity and manhood, in very different ways, through difficult personal struggle.

**SOURCES FOR FURTHER STUDY**

Carelton, Mark T. *Politics and Punishment: The History of the Louisiana State Penal System*. Baton Rouge: Louisiana State University Press, 1971.

Kenney, W. P. "*A Lesson Before Dying*, by Ernest J. Gaines." In *Masterplots II: African American Fiction Series*, edited by Frank N. Magill. Vol. 2. Pasadena, Calif.: Salem Press, 1994.

Woodson, Jacqueline. *A Way Out of No Way: Writings About Growing Up Black in America*. New York: Fawcett Juniper, 1996.

# Other Works

**CATHERINE CARMIER** (1964). Ernest J. Gaines's first published novel, *Catherine Carmier*, is a love story of forbidden romance modeled on the nineteenth-century Russian novelist Ivan Turgenev's *Fathers and Sons*. The characters in *Catherine Carmier* face changes in things over which they have little control and must make difficult decisions without strong guidance. Personal strength and moral convictions are tested, but Gaines is more concerned with how decisions are made than with whether they have been made properly. The central problems of the story—tension between the generations in rural communities and the devastation caused by rigid class and racial rules—are favorite themes to which Gaines returned frequently in later works.

Jackson, a young black man, returns to rural Louisiana after attending college in California, where he has gained new experience and values. Jackson's education has helped him reject the traditional racial prejudices still in place in the rural South. He symbolizes new ways of thinking. Jackson falls in love with the light-skinned Catherine, the daughter of Raoul, a black Creole sharecropper. Catherine's father isolates her, believing that he is protecting her from darker-skinned people of lower social status.

Catherine is loyal to her father but also begins to love Jackson. She is torn between her loyalty to her father and tradition, her identity as an African American, and her love for Jackson. Raoul and Jackson finally clash violently, and Raoul is beaten. Catherine tells Jackson to go but promises she will meet him. The story ends with Jackson waiting and wondering whether Catherine will appear.

*Catherine Carmier* received little positive notice, but critics suggested that it showed Gaines's promise as a writer. Gaines was criticized for excluding contemporary political views from his work, which was published during the years of the Civil Rights movement. The novel is generally considered the least characteristic of Gaines's work.

**IN MY FATHER'S HOUSE** (1978). Gaines's fourth novel takes place in an urban rather than a rural setting. In it, Gaines explores the alienation of black fathers and sons through the devastating effects of a father's abandonment of his children and his fear of accepting the responsibilities of manhood.

Philip Martin is a respected preacher and a civil rights activist. He is confronted by an angry young stranger named Robert X, who is eventually revealed to be his son from a relationship with a woman many years before. Robert X is hostile and bitter. He wants to kill Martin for leaving his mother and her three children in poverty and for the suffering they have endured without a father's protection.

Gaines is concerned with the socially and emotionally crippling legacy of slavery on African American culture. The social codes of the South have engendered discrimination and hostility toward African Americans, particularly toward men, who are considered inferior as well as threatening. Because of this legacy, Gaines's characters often lack self-respect and remain passive against constant degradation. They have learned self-hatred, which destroys them if they cannot somehow regain pride and dignity.

The confrontation with his previously unknown son forces Martin into a long and painful search for his lost family, as he tries to find both the truth about the past and the consequences of his irresponsible actions. Robert X's bitterness and anger make communication with his father impossible. Consumed with rage, pain, and despair, Robert X commits suicide. Here Gaines seems to imply that human actions are determined by the past. Martin has sacrificed his comfortable life to try to rebuild the old, but it is too late. His family needed him, but his choice to leave destroyed them. Martin's quest touches on the issues of personal responsibility and is really the search for manhood in a world that can be guided no longer by the wisdom of the past. It is a common journey for the male characters in the work of Ernest J. Gaines.

# *Resources*

The main collection of Ernest J. Gaines's manuscripts is located at Dupree Library, University of Southwestern Louisiana, Lafayette. Other sources of interest to students of Gaines include the following:

**Special Journal Issue.** A special issue of the literary journal *Callaloo* 1, no. 3 (1978), published by the department of English at the University of Kentucky in Lexington, is devoted to Ernest J. Gaines and includes a checklist of criticism through 1977.

**Audio Recordings.** The American Audio Prose Library has published audiocassette recordings (1986) of Ernest Gaines's interview with Kay Bonetti and his reading of excerpts from *A Gathering of Old Men*. As part of a series called *New Letters on the Air* (1989), for the Kansas City, Missouri, magazine *New Letters*, Gaines reads from his collection of short stories, *Bloodline*. He also talks about his life.

**Video Recordings.** *Louisiana Legends: Ernest J. Gaines*, produced by Louisiana Public Broadcasting in 1982, is an interview with Ernest Gaines by Gus Weill. Also of interest is *Louisiana Stories*, produced in 1992 by the Louisiana Educational Television Authority.

*MARGARET E. PARKS*

# John Gardner

**BORN:** July 21, 1933, Batavia, New York
**DIED:** September 14, 1982, Susquehanna, Pennsylvania
**IDENTIFICATION:** Prolific novelist, short-story writer, scholar, and literary critic who combined realism, symbolism, and morality into a distinctive artistic vision.

Active as a scholar and a poet, John Gardner assured his position as a major writer of fiction with works such as *October Light* (1976) while stirring controversy with his polemical, highly personal criticism of contemporary authors in his frankly opinionated volume *On Moral Fiction* (1978). *The Sunlight Dialogues* (1972), by general consensus Gardner's most impressive work, combined the traditional sweep of generational novels with the experimental techniques of postmodernist writers. Gardner published his most important works during the ten years prior to his untimely accidental death in 1982. Many observers believe that the reception by critics and the literary establishment of his later works suffered as a result, but there is no doubt that his enduring accomplishments and legacy remain.

# The Writer's Life

John Champlin Gardner, Jr., was born on July 21, 1933, in Batavia, in western New York State. His father was a dairy farmer and a lay preacher, and his mother was an English teacher. Both of his parents were artistically inclined, and Gardner later credited them as an important early influence on his work.

**Childhood Trauma.** The defining moment in Gardner's life—what he would later refer to as his "writer's wound"—happened on April 4, 1945, when he was eleven years old. Gardner was driving a large farm tractor pulling a two-ton roller known as a cultipacker. His younger brother, Gilbert, was sitting behind on the crossbar that linked the cultipacker to the tractor. As the tractor came over a hill, it suddenly stopped, throwing Gilbert to the ground. Before Gardner could react, the heavy cultipacker had rolled over his younger brother, crushing his skull and killing him instantly.

Gardner felt he had killed his brother. Later, when he realized it had been an accident, he was profoundly troubled by the paradox of a supposedly loving God who might have willed Gilbert's death. The only other possibility was that his brother had died by mere chance, suggesting that human life was without meaning. As a writer, Gardner returned obsessively to the idea of meaning versus chance.

This photograph of Gardner was taken by his son, Joel, in 1982, the same year Gardner was killed in a motorcycle accident. Gardner was the quintessential renaissance man. As well as writing novels, poems, and plays, he translated medieval texts, composed operas and librettos, played the French horn, and was an avid painter.

## Student and Teacher.

After graduating from Batavia High School, Gardner attended DePauw University for two years. He married Joan Louise Patterson in 1953, and the couple later had two children, Joel and Lucy. Also in 1953, Gardner transferred to Washington University in St. Louis, graduating two years later as a member of Phi Beta Kappa. He next attended the University of Iowa on a Woodrow Wilson Fellowship, submitting a novel, "The Old Men," as his 1958 doctoral dissertation.

Gardner had made Old English, Anglo-Saxon, and medieval literature his field of specialty, and he soon taught briefly at Oberlin College, Chico State College, and San Francisco State College. In September 1965 he became an associate professor of English at Southern Illinois University in Carbondale, where he would remain until 1974, teaching Anglo-Saxon and medieval studies. He edited scholarly works, including *The Complete Works of the Gawain-Poet* (1965), which was praised for its poetic rendition but faulted for its idiosyncratic interpretations. Gardner was also writing his own creative works, both poetry and prose, and working on the literary magazine *MSS*.

As Gardner gained prominence as a writer, he left Southern Illinois for brief stays at Bennington College, Williams College, Skidmore College, and George Mason University. In 1978 he accepted a position at the State University of New York at Binghamton, where he taught in the school's creative writing program until his death.

Gardner felt an affinity for the writings of fourteenth-century poet Geoffrey Chaucer. In the early 1960s he completed a thousand-page study of Chaucer's life and works.

## A Writing Career Begins.

Gardner began his creative writing early. Portions of *Nickel Mountain: A Pastoral Novel*, which was published in 1973, were composed when the author was only nineteen, and some of them had appeared in a student literary magazine in 1955. Early drafts of novels that would later appear in print included *The Resurrection* (1966) and *The Sunlight Dialogues*. It was not until 1966, however, with *The Resurrection*, that Gardner at last became a published novelist.

*The Resurrection*'s debut passed almost without notice. It was followed in 1970 by *The*

*Wreckage of Agathon*, which attracted more interest, perhaps because the novel's theme of the individual versus the authority of the state echoed the temper of a United States deeply divided over the Vietnam War. Gardner's next novel, *Grendel* (1971), made a major impact on both critics and the public. The monster-hero Grendel was compared to King Kong, John Milton's Lucifer, and William Shakespeare's Caliban.

## The Turning Point.

In 1972 Gardner published *The Sunlight Dialogues*. The long, densely packed, highly intellectual novel spent fifteen weeks on the best-seller list of *The New York Times* and won considerable acclaim. The novel was compared to Herman Melville's *Moby Dick* (1851). Gardner himself was likened to the novelist William Faulkner. *Time's* review, making a favorable comparison with James Joyce's masterpiece, said that the novel's ending monologue "caps and shapes the book as Molly Bloom's soliloquy shapes and caps *Ulysses*."

Gardner's career dipped with the publication of *Jason and Medeia* (1973), a verse retelling of the myth of the Golden Fleece, but *Nickel Mountain* and *The King's Indian: Stories and Tales* (1974) proved that Gardner had mastery of traditional narrative fiction, as well as "metafiction," fiction that discusses itself while telling the story. *Nickel Mountain* and *The King's Indian* were masterpieces of their respective genres. The first returned Gardner to the best-seller lists, while the second established him as one of the most innovative and skillful new American writers.

In 1976 Gardner published what he called his "bicentennial novel," *October Light*, about the rebellion of an elderly woman against her tyrannical brother in upstate Vermont. The setting was by then familiar to Gardner, as he was teaching at Bennington College in Bennington, Vermont. *October Light* was Gardner's last major critical and popular success: a best-seller that garnered favorable reviews and received the National Book Critics Circle Award for outstanding fiction, which many observers considered postdated recognition for *The Sunlight Dialogues*.

## Controversy, Rejection, and Death.

In 1977 Gardner's personal and professional lives were in turmoil. Going through a difficult divorce, battling both the IRS and colon cancer, he was further besieged by charges of plagiarism, poor scholarship, and faulty interpretations in his dual critical and biographical studies, *The Poetry of Chaucer* and *The Life and Times of Chaucer*, both published in that year.

Worse followed with the publication of *On Moral Fiction* in 1978. In this work, Gardner called writers to create serious art rather than literary games and insisted on artistic standards that affirmed the best aspects of human nature—while not glossing over the harsh realities of life. Gardner argued that literature was an important aspect of actual life. Critical response was highly negative, dismissing Gardner's views as cranky, rhetorical and, worst of all, old-fashioned.

Critics used *On Moral Fiction* as a guide not only for Gardner's subsequent works but also for his earlier ones, as they searched for, and found, moralizing tenets in the Sunlight Man's dialogues or ethical ruminations in Agathon's rantings. *Freddy's Book* (1980), the short-story collection *The Art of Living and Other Stories* (1981), and Gardner's final novel, *Mickelsson's Ghosts* (1982), were castigated for what many perceived as their preachy and moralistic tone. *Freddy's Book* in particular, with its grotesque main character and supernatural novel-within-a-novel, was unfavorably compared to *Grendel*. *Mickelsson's Ghosts* was slighted by reference to *The Sunlight Dialogues*.

Four days before his planned third marriage, John Gardner lost control of his Harley-Davidson motorcycle on a curving highway three miles from his home in Susquehanna, Pennsylvania, and was killed. He was forty-nine years old.

# HIGHLIGHTS IN GARDNER'S LIFE

**1933**      John Champlin Gardner, Jr., is born on July 21 in Batavia, New York.

**1945**      Younger brother, Gilbert, is killed in a farm accident.

**1951**      Gardner graduates from Batavia High School; enters DePauw University.

**1953**      Marries Joan Louise Patterson; transfers to Washington University.

**1955**      Graduates from Washington University, Phi Beta Kappa; enters University of Iowa.

**1958**      Receives doctorate from University of Iowa.

**1956–1965** Teaches at various colleges and universities.

**1965**      Becomes associate professor of English at Southern Illinois University-Carbondale.

**1966**      Publishes first novel, *The Resurrection*.

**1971**      Publishes *Grendel*; begins to receive critical attention.

**1972**      Publishes *The Sunlight Dialogues*, his breakthrough novel.

**1974**      Publishes *The King's Indian*, a book of short fiction.

**1976**      Publishes novel *October Light*; receives National Book Critics Circle Award for fiction.

**1977**      Divorces his wife; is successfully treated for colon cancer.

**1977**      Publishes biography and critical study of Chaucer; is accused of plagiarism and shoddy scholarship.

**1978**      Joins faculty of State University of New York at Binghamton.

**1978**      Publishes *On Moral Fiction*, stirring intense controversy.

**1980**      Publishes *Freddy's Book*.

**1981**      Publishes *The Art of Living and Other Stories*.

**1982**      Publishes *Mickelsson's Ghosts*, with photographs by his son, Joel.

**1982**      Dies in a motorcycle accident in Susquehanna, Pennsylvania, on September 14.

**1986**      *"Stillness" and "Shadows"* is edited and published by Nicholas Delbanco.

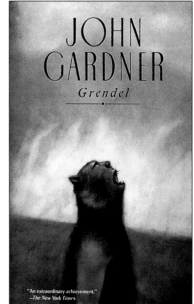

# The Writer's Work

John Gardner was a prolific writer in a wide variety of genres and works, ranging from original long fiction to translations of ancient Greek epic poetry. He is best known and most widely respected for his realistic novels of contemporary American life, filled with a wide variety of believable characters. These novels generally have a philosophical and moral undercurrent.

**Gardner, Realism, and Parody.** Gardner's writings were a complex and paradoxical combination of realism and parody. *The Sunlight Dialogues* is an excellent example of this combination on a large scale. The work is clearly grounded in realism, with the locale of Batavia being firmly and deftly established as an actual location in the contemporary world. The char-

acters, from Chief Clumly on, have a solid heft and weight—sometimes literally so—that establishes them as three-dimensional. Clearly, the novel is, at least on one level, a work of consummate realism.

At the same time *The Sunlight Dialogues* also contains broad strokes of parody and comedy that border on the farcical. The Sunlight Man is a larger-than-life character—almost a cartoon figure—who can perform amazing and magical feats with effortless ease. Chief Clumly, large, pale, and totally hairless, is rescued from being an unbelievably grotesque figure only by Gardner's skill in crafting him as an odd, but distinctly human, individual. In a similar fashion much of the novel's action, especially the dialogues between the Sunlight Man and Chief Clumly, are in and of themselves absurd. In real life, such conversations would not—in fact, could not—occur as they do. However, Gardner's skill is such that he can create what he once called the goal of all great writing, "a vivid and sustained dream."

Although this mixture of realism and parody is found in all of Gardner's fiction, it is most evident in *The King's Indian*. Here, Gardner literally takes off on two classics of American literature, Melville's *Moby Dick* and Edgar Allen Poe's *The Narrative of Arthur Gordon Pym* (1838) to create a sly, multireferential tale

Robert Sholties's 1998 acrylic painting *Winter Games* captures the blend of realism and parody that is one of the hallmarks of Gardner's work. In *The Sunlight Dialogues*, offbeat and comical characters inhabit a fictional world based on the novelist's hometown of Batavia, New York, located in a region known for its often-brutal winters.

Gardner gained inspiration from a wide variety of sources, most notably philosophy; the animated films of Walt Disney; and ancient myths and literature, especially Old English, Anglo-Saxon, and medieval writing, which were his areas of academic specialty. Clear indications of all of these sources are found throughout his works. In *The Sunlight Dialogues*, for example, ancient Babylonian myths are a key structural motif while many of the broadly sketched characters are essentially cartoonlike figures. In *The King's Indian*, Gardner conducts an ongoing conversation with numerous great American writers, most notably Melville and Poe. In many places, Gardner paraphrases or even quotes from these authors.

Philosophy was an ongoing interest—some might say obsession—with Gardner. Many of his novels are overtly philosophical: *The Resurrection*, *The Wreckage of Agathon*, and *Mickelsson's Ghosts* are literally about philosophers coming to accept their own mortality. *The Sunlight Dialogues* and *Nickel Mountain* both contain many philosophical discussions that use everyday language to address fundamental issues.

Finally, in the settings for his writings Gardner returned repeatedly to the area where he was born and raised: upstate New York. The state's western mountains and valleys serve as the backdrop for both *Nickel Mountain* and *Mickelsson's Ghosts*, and his hometown of Batavia is featured in *The Sunlight Dialogues*.

that continually nudges the reader, and itself, with hints, allusions, and illusions. Sometimes, the narrator is Jonathan Upchurch, the main character in the novel. At other times, the narrator is Gardner himself, who pauses to address the reader directly, making the earnest point that the novel is not "one more trick of exhausted art" right before embarking on another display of authorial trickery. The drollery continues even in the volume's illustrations by Herbert L. Fink; the portrait of Jonathan Upchurch is clearly John Gardner himself.

**Gardner and Moral Fiction.** In 1965, before Gardner was published as a novelist, he began writing a work that appeared in 1978 as *On Moral Fiction*. This volume presented both Gardner's assessments of his fellow novelists and his deeply felt theoretical basis for literature and, in fact, all art. His opinions on the former caused intense controversy and negatively affected the critical reception of his own fiction, while his opinions on the latter were largely ignored in the subsequent debate.

Gardner's position was quite simple, indeed traditional: Art, particularly literature, affects the way people behave. If art is superficial and cynical, then readers and, by extension, society, will become that way also. Therefore it is the role of true writers to craft "moral fiction." Moral fiction captures the essence of life in a positive, life-affirming fashion. Gardner believed that traditional Western realism is the vehicle best suited for this purpose. He argued that the fascination with form, texture, and metafiction—stories about stories, or about writers writing about writing—that had replaced realism reflected the bankrupt nature of contemporary writing. He believed that authors such as Donald Barthelme, John Barth, and Thomas Pynchon were symptomatic of this pervasive problem.

Critics of *On Moral Fiction* reacted negatively to both the commentary on specific authors and the emphatic, even belligerent, tone. Gardner's subsequent novels were reviewed and dismissed as examples of didactic moral fiction, and his earlier works were negatively reexamined as well. However, such revisionist views missed the point: Gardner had always believed that art had a moral purpose, but that purpose, important though it was, was always secondary to art's impact on the reader. For John Gardner, literature was both inherently playful and intensely serious.

## BIBLIOGRAPHY

Butts, Leonard. *The Novels of John Gardner: Making Life Art as a Moral Process.* Baton Rouge: University of Louisiana Press, 1988.

Cowart, David. *Arches and Light: The Fiction of John Gardner.* Carbondale: Southern Illinois University Press, 1983.

Henderson, Jeff. *John Gardner: A Study of the Short Fiction.* Boston: Twayne Publishers, 1990.

Howell, John. *Understanding John Gardner.* Columbia: University of South Carolina Press, 1993.

McWilliams, Dean. *John Gardner.* Boston: Twayne Publishers, 1990.

Morris, Gregory. *A World of Order and Light: The Fiction of John Gardner.* Athens: University of Georgia Press, 1984.

Nutter, Ronald. *A Dream of Peace: Art and Death in the Fiction of John Gardner.* Vol. 9 in *Modern American Literature, New Approaches.* New York: Peter Lang, 1997.

Winther, Per. *The Art of John Gardner: Instruction and Exploration.* Albany: State University of New York Press, 1992.

## LONG FICTION

| 1966 | The Resurrection |
| 1970 | The Wreckage of Agathon |
| 1971 | Grendel |
| 1972 | The Sunlight Dialogues |
| 1973 | Nickel Mountain: A Pastoral Novel |
| 1976 | October Light |
| 1977 | In the Suicide Mountains |
| 1980 | Freddy's Book |
| 1982 | Mickelsson's Ghosts |
| 1986 | "Stillness" and "Shadows" (with Nicholas Delbanco) |

## SHORT FICTION

| 1974 | The King's Indian: Stories and Tales |
| 1981 | The Art of Living and Other Stories |

## POETRY

| 1973 | Jason and Medeia |
| 1978 | Poems |

## PLAYS AND OPERA LIBRETTOS

| 1977 | The Temptation Game (radio play) |
| 1979 | Death and the Maiden |
| 1979 | Frankenstein (libretto) |
| 1979 | Rumpelstiltskin (libretto) |
| 1979 | William Wilson (libretto) |

## NONFICTION

| 1974 | The Construction of the Wakefield Cycle |
| 1975 | The Construction of Christian Poetry in Old English |
| 1977 | The Poetry of Chaucer |
| 1977 | The Life and Times of Chaucer |
| 1978 | On Moral Fiction |
| 1983 | On Becoming a Novelist |
| 1984 | The Art of Fiction: Notes on Craft for Young Writers |

## EDITED TEXTS

| 1962 | The Forms of Fiction (with Lennis Dunlap) |
| 1965 | The Complete Works of the Gawain-Poet |
| 1967 | Papers on the Art and Age of Geoffrey Chaucer (with Nicholas Joost) |
| 1971 | The Alliterative "Morte d' Arthure," "The Owl and the Nightingale," and Five Other Middle English Poems |

## CHILDREN'S LITERATURE

| 1975 | Dragon, Dragon and Other Tales |
| 1976 | Gudgekin the Thistle Girl and Other Tales |
| 1977 | A Child's Bestiary |
| 1977 | The King of the Hummingbirds and Other Tales |

## TRANSLATION

| 1984 | Gilgamesh (with John Maier) |

# Reader's Guide to Major Works

**GRENDEL**

> **Genre:** Novel
> **Subgenre:** Historical fantasy
> **Published:** New York, 1971
> **Time period:** Sixth century
> **Setting:** Denmark

**Themes and Issues.** The underlying theme of *Grendel* is the place of the individual in the universe, and the fundamental issue is whether there is any overriding reason to that universe. In a sense, *Grendel* is a philosophical novel that uses Anglo-Saxon characters to confront modern existentialist thinkers, in particular the French author Jean-Paul Sartre.

The monster Grendel embodies the quality of alienation—a conscious sense of isolation—because, for all he knows, he and his mother are the only of all their kind in the world. He is both drawn to and repelled by the world of human beings. He is fascinated by the poetry of the blind singer, Shaper, yet repulsed by the mindless violence of Hrothgar and his noble thanes. Before he knew human beings, Grendel

Gardner's protagonists, such as Grendel, the title character of Gardner's 1971 fantasy novel, are often forced to come to grips with their sense of isolation in the world. The solitary figure in Hughie Lee-Smith's oil painting *The Stranger* (The Smithsonian American Art Museum, Washington, D.C.) reflects Grendel's loneliness.

killed only for food; after his exposure to the Danes, he kills for revenge and for other motives he cannot even name.

Such is the essential dilemma of human beings. They aspire to the highest ideals, such as those given artistic life by Shaper. At the same time, they descend with frightening rapidity into brute savagery. Grendel, just outside humanity, is a baffled but objective observer to this situation. Because Grendel is conscious but not human, he is able to articulate—though not resolve—the paradox that is human life.

**The Plot.** John Gardner's *Grendel* is a retelling of the Old English poem *Beowulf* (ca. 1000) from the monster's point of view. The strange creature Grendel and his mother live alone on the borders of the kingdom of Hrothgar, the aging king of the Danes. For twelve years a war has raged between the Danes and Grendel because they have rejected him out of fear and loathing. Lured by the seductive rhymes of Shaper, the blind poet who is part of Hrothgar's court, Grendel yearns to be friends with humans and share their dreams, but he rejects their bloody, pointless ways.

Grendel is troubled by the suspicion that there may be no order or plan to the universe, and this fear is underscored when he encounters an ancient, wise, and evil dragon who confirms the pointless nature of reality. The dragon is a prophet of nihilism and pure chance who inspires Grendel to intensify his attacks on the Danes. Finally, the mighty Danish hero Beowulf arrives to hunt down Grendel and destroy him. Grendel is strangely fascinated by Beowulf, even drawn to him, but when they inevitably meet, Beowulf tears off Grendel's arm and the monster flees into the darkness.

**Analysis.** In *Grendel* Gardner took the Beowulf story and retold it from the monster's point of view. In doing so, he fashioned a remarkably original novel that brought him his first sustained and serious attention from both critics and the reading public. *Grendel* distinguished Gardner as one of the promi-

nent voices of late-twentieth-century American literature. The most remarkable thing about the novel is its narrative voice, which is that of Grendel himself. At times the creature speaks with the assured assonance of Anglo-Saxon alliteration, and the text even quotes or at least paraphrases from the original. At other points the tone is more modern, even colloquial, giving a sense of immediacy and presence. The combination of the two voices makes *Grendel* seem less the memory of an ancient myth than a first-hand report of a story that is still unfolding in a distant but contemporary land whose inhabitants may be strange but are immediately recognizable.

## SOURCES FOR FURTHER STUDY

Fawcet, Barry, and Elizabeth Jones. "The Twelve Traps in John Gardner's *Grendel*." *American Literature* 62 (1990).

Moor, Judy Smith. "John Gardner's Order and Disorder: *Grendel* and *The Sunlight Dialogues*." *Critique: Studies in Modern Fiction* 8, no. 4 (1976).

Payne, Craig. "The Cycle of the Zodiac in John Gardner's *Grendel*." *Mythlore* 67 (1991).

Segedy, Michael. "A Critical Look at John Gardner's *Grendel*." *Virginia English Bulletin* 36, no. 2 (1982).

Stromme, Craig. "The Twelve Chapters of *Grendel*." *Critique: Studies in Modern Fiction* 20, no. 1 (1978).

## OCTOBER LIGHT

**Genre:** Novel
**Subgenre:** Realism
**Published:** New York, 1976
**Time period:** 1976
**Setting:** Dairy farm near Bennington, Vermont

**Themes and Issues.** Published in 1976, *October Light* was John Gardner's "bicentennial novel." James Page, the intolerant brother, could be seen to represent Great Britain and Sally, his sister, the American colonies. The novel makes frequent references, directly and indirectly, to the American Revolution and its leaders and finds counterpoints to their actions in the activities of James and Sally.

Edward Hopper's 1950 oil painting *Cape Cod Morning* (The Smithsonian American Art Museum, Washington, D.C.) suggests the isolation of Sally, the character who shut herself off from the world, living in a self-imposed exile in her room in Gardner's 1976 novel, *October Light*.

The themes of the past and, more specifically, of guilt and redemption for past actions are woven throughout the book. All of the novel's characters are haunted, to a greater or lesser degree, by a sense of the past. Some of them, most notably James Page, are emotionally bound by a sense of guilt for accidents, misfortunes, and deaths. It is only at the novel's end that, through the power of love, the characters become unbound, much as the Vermont landscape comes to life in the spring after the long prison of winter.

**The Plot.** After her husband's death, Sally Page Abbott comes to live with her brother, James Page, on his dairy farm near Bennington, Vermont. She brings a television, enraging her brother, who blasts it with his shotgun. A week later, angered at Sally's liberal ideas, James chases her to her bedroom. Sally locks herself in for a hunger strike, although she finds and makes free use of several bushels of apples stored in the attic.

While locked in her bedroom, Sally discovers a discarded paperback novel, *The Smugglers of Lost Souls' Rock,* which she begins to read.

She is soon fascinated, almost against her will, by the trashy novel. Meanwhile, James is haunted by guilt—his youngest son, Ethan, fell to his death from the barn and his eldest son, Richard, hanged himself—and his emotions keep him from reaching out to his sister. It is only toward the end of the novel, when both siblings have faced the past and its sorrows, that they can be reconciled.

**Analysis.** Since one of the major characters is locked in a room throughout most of the novel and the other is a cranky old man who hates modern life, much of the action in *October Light* takes place in these characters' minds and memories. Sally and James constantly refer back to the past, reliving most often its pains and disappointments, unable to move beyond them.

In a similar fashion, the novel-within-a-novel that Sally reads in her room helps to create a sort of closed system. The absurd events of the pulp fiction trigger more serious and profound reflections, both in Sally as she reads *The Smugglers of Lost Souls' Rock* and in the readers of *October Light*. In this sense, *October Light* becomes an elaborate metafiction that plays on the roles and realities of literature at the same time it deconstructs them.

### SOURCES FOR FURTHER STUDY

Allen, Bruce. "Settling for Ithaca: The Fictions of John Gardner." *Sewanee Review* 85 (1977).

Butts, Leonard. "Locking and Unlocking: Nature as Moral Center in John Gardner's *October Light*." *Critique: Studies in Modern Fiction* 22, no. 2 (1980).

Cowart, David. "The Dying Fall in John Gardner's *October Light*." *Twentieth-Century Literature* 29 (1983).

## THE SUNLIGHT DIALOGUES

**Genre:** Novel
**Subgenre:** Realism
**Published:** New York, 1972
**Time period:** August, 1966
**Setting:** Batavia, New York

**Themes and Issues.** In this complex philosophical novel, Gardner contrasts issues of individual freedom with issues of community order. The unlikely spokespersons for these two competing visions are the Sunlight Man, part anarchist and part magician, and a small-town chief of police whose main desire is to lead a quiet life. The two men explore most, if not all, of the ramifications of these enduring philosophical divisions, relating to them both as timeless puzzles and as practical problems in the modern world.

**The Plot.** The novel's central characters are Batavia chief of police Fred Clumly and an unnamed, bearded individual known as the Sunlight Man. When Clumly arrests the Sunlight Man for painting the word *Love* on a

Gardner elegantly renders the details of small-town life, captured here in Anthony Brunelli's 1995 oil painting *Walter's Shoes*, in his novel *The Sunlight Dialogues*. Gardner's finely crafted details provide a realistic backdrop for the action of the novel.

street, the new prisoner soon has the jail in turmoil with his continual speeches questioning all authority, human and divine. The Sunlight Man escapes with another prisoner, and a guard is killed—the first of several deaths caused by the Sunlight Man. Clumly sets off in dogged pursuit.

Intuitively, Clumly believes that the town's most prominent family, the Hodges, are somehow connected with the Sunlight Man. He is correct; the man is in fact Taggert Hodge, who left town sixteen years earlier after his insane wife burned down their house, killing their two sons. Now the Sunlight Man stalks and captures Millie, his brother Will's ex-wife. He is determined to transform the vain, selfish Millie into a saint—possibly to redeem her and possibly to salvage part of his own past.

Throughout the novel, Clumly and the Sunlight Man meet in places around Batavia to engage in the philosophical dialogues that give the novel its title. The two men discuss fundamental divisions: the desire for order versus the yearning for freedom; the good of the community versus the rights of the individual; and the enduring struggle of good versus evil. Clumly, although a relatively untutored individual, manages through his very simplicity and stubborn integrity to be a match for the Sunlight Man.

While Clumly grows intellectually and spiritually, his tangible world disintegrates around him. His obsession with the Sunlight Man disturbs his blind wife, Esther, and angers the mayor and town council, who eventually remove him from office. At a last meeting at Stony Hill, the Hodges' historic mansion, Clumly and the Sunlight Man come to an understanding. Burning Stony Hill as atonement for and exorcism of his past, the Sunlight Man comes into town to surrender, only to be shot—significantly, through the heart—by a startled policeman.

**Analysis.** *The Sunlight Dialogues* is the high point of Gardner's fiction. It successfully blends his philosophical, ethical, and moral concerns with well-created and believable characters who inhabit a world that is immediately and lastingly real. Gardner uses, as he often does, the upstate New York area where he was raised to assist in creating a real, recognizable setting for the action and discussion. He embodies the abstract philosophical dialogues in the concrete persons of Clumly and the Sunlight Man. This was Gardner's goal in most, if not all, of his novels, and it is achieved most fully in *The Sunlight Dialogues*.

*The Sunlight Dialogues* was the first of Gardner's books to achieve popular acclaim. It spent a number of weeks on several best-seller lists and established him as a novelist who was not afraid to tackle serious issues in a long and complex narrative. It is filled with deep and searching philosophical questions, a considerable amount of action, and an extensive gallery of memorable, highly individualized characters. It is the successful combination of these seemingly disparate features that has established *The Sunlight Dialogues* as Gardner's greatest fictional accomplishment.

## SOURCES FOR FURTHER STUDY

Bellamy, Joe David, and Pat Ensworth. "John Gardner." In *The New Fiction: Interviews with Innovative American Writers*, edited by Joe David Bellamy. Urbana: University of Illinois Press, 1974.

Fredrickson, Robert. "Losing Battles Against Entropy: *The Sunlight Dialogues*." *Modern Language Studies* 13 (1983).

Moor, Judy Smith. "John Gardner's Order and Disorder: *Grendel* and *The Sunlight Dialogues*." *Critique: Studies in Modern Fiction* 18, no. 2 (1976).

Morace, Robert. "*The Sunlight Dialogues*: A Giant (Paperback) Leap Backwards." *Notes on Contemporary Literature* 8, no. 4 (1978).

Morris, Greg. "A Babylonian in Batavia: Mesopotamian Literature and Lore in *The Sunlight Dialogues*." In *John Gardner: Critical Perspectives*, edited by Robert A. Morace and Kathryn VanSpanckeren. Carbondale: Southern Illinois University Press, 1982.

Payne, Alison. "Clown, Monster, Magician: The Purpose of Lunacy in John Gardner's Fiction." In *Thor's Hammer*, edited by Jeff Henderson. Conway: University of Central Arkansas Press, 1985.

# Other Works

**THE KING'S INDIAN: STORIES AND TALES** (1974). *The King's Indian* is a rich collection that deals with the relationship between life and art. The work is divided into three "books." "The Midnight Reader" consists of Gothic and supernatural stories. "Tales of Queen Louisa" is a set of stories centered around a mad queen and her surreal court. The novella "The King's Indian: A Tale" is the centerpiece of the book.

"The King's Indian" is an elaborate literary concoction in which an Illinois farm boy, Jonathan Upchurch, finds himself on a mysterious vessel mastered by Captain Flint. Flint bears more than a passing resemblance to *Moby Dick*'s Captain Ahab. As the ship sails south toward the Vanishing Isles, literary echoes abound, from poet Samuel Taylor Coleridge's Ancient Mariner to Poe's Arthur Gordon Pym. At times, John Gardner breaks from his narrative to directly address the reader, reinforcing the fact that this work is metafiction carried to its ultimate extreme.

**NICKEL MOUNTAIN: A PASTORAL NOVEL** (1973). Set in a small community in New York's Catskill Mountains, *Nickel Mountain* emphasizes the transcendent powers of goodness and love. The central character is Henry Soames, who owns the Stop-Off Café. Henry is troubled—literally and figuratively—by heart problems, but these begin to be resolved when he marries Callie Wells, a sixteen-year-old waitress left pregnant by her boyfriend. As Henry finds a new life with Callie and her son, he brings life to his community as a figure of love, tolerance, and wisdom.

The novel's subtitle, *A Pastoral Novel*, is a typical Gardnerian play on words. In one sense, it is literally a pastoral, set in the countryside and concerned with farmers and their families. The natural rhythm of the year's seasons governs the story's action. In another sense, Henry Soames is like a pastor to the small community in which he lives. He is often compared to Jesus in the narrative and acts as a sort of "good shepherd" to Callie, Jimmy, and his neighbors.

**ON MORAL FICTION** (1978). In *On Moral Fiction* Gardner sets forth—clearly, coherently, and perhaps even a bit stridently—the philosophical foundations of his fiction. He draws a distinction between himself and other contemporary writers that finds them lacking in the

*Paul's Magic*, a 1977 oil painting by James Valerio, depicts elements of the surreal. Such elements reflect the very nature of Gardner's writing. "I think that fantasy . . . is the mainstream of literature from the beginning," he once said.

moral seriousness needed for true art. His assessment so enraged the literary establishment that his subsequent career was seriously affected.

True moral art, according to Gardner, affirms and reinforces the dignity and purpose of human life while avoiding cheap sentimentality. Moral art is both realistic and educational: It shows how human beings are and teaches them how they should be. *On Moral Fiction* offers a sustained, organized exposition of Gardner's philosophy of what constitutes good and lasting art, in particular literary art, while revealing the fundamental framework of his own fictions.

**THE RESURRECTION**(1966). The first of Gardner's novels to be published, *The Resurrection* was actually written after he had completed drafts of *Nickel Mountain* and *The Sunlight Dialogues*. Like *The Sunlight Dialogues*, *The Resurrection* is a "philosophical novel," in which its characters openly confront and discuss timeless issues such as faith, love, and the affirmation of life in the face of death.

The plot of *The Resurrection* is simple: James Chandler, a professor of philosophy, learns that he has a terminal disease that gives him less than a month to live and returns to his hometown of Batavia, New York. He meets the mysteriously beautiful nineteen-year-old Viola Staley and believes he has fallen in love with her. After a series of philosophical discussions with various characters, Chandler drags himself from his hospital bed to the Staley house, literally dying at Viola's feet.

*The Resurrection*'s technique is reminiscent of a Socratic dialogue. Gardner's ear for dialect and individual expression is evident; however, the exchanges are far from naturalistic, especially those between James Chandler and his fellow patient John Horne, a grotesquely fat man with a brilliant, but skewed, mind. In the end, love redeems all and is symbolized by the four women who visit Chandler's grave: his mother, wife, daughter, and Viola Staley.

Gardner's writing always expressed an abiding respect for human dignity. *The Blue Collar World of Joe Wong,* a 1999 oil painting by Charles S. Jarboe, presents a man content with all that lies before him.

**THE WRECKAGE OF AGATHON** (1970). In ancient Greece, Agathon is an ironic counterpart to Socrates. He bedevils the upright citizens of conformist Sparta—especially their legendary lawgiver, Lykourgos—by continually questioning authority in his erratic, maddening quest for truth.

The novel unfolds in chapters narrated by Agathon and Demodokos, Agathon's only disciple, known as Peeker. Agathon is vain and self-centered; he blusters and pontificates his way through the story as through his life, provoking and challenging the reader as he does the authorities. Peeker perceives the situation with commonsense practicality: He and Agathon are in the grasp of an inflexible system that demands order and sees Agathon as a threat. Therefore, Agathon must submit or die. At the novel's end, Agathon dies and Peeker survives, suggesting that Peeker will be the better philosopher.

## *Resources*

For the student of John Gardner, there are three major collections of materials about his life and work and several Web sites that provide information about his life, career, and influence.

**The Nicholas Joost Papers and the Kenneth Aguillard Atchity Collection.** Both these collections are housed at the Georgetown University Library in Washington, D.C. Joost, the editor of several literary journals, including *Poetry*, was a close correspondent with many modern American writers, among them Gardner. His collection contains a wealth of Gardner information. Atchity, an avid student of contemporary American literature, also corresponded freely with numerous authors, including Gardner.

**The John Gardner Archive.** The largest single collection of manuscripts by, and relating to, John Gardner, the John Gardner Archive is housed at the Rush Rhees Library at the University of Rochester in Rochester, New York. The collection includes papers, materials, and other resources. The archive maintains an extensive and useful Web site. (http://www.lib.rochester.edu/rbk/Gardner3.htm)

**The Arch and the Abyss: A John C. Gardner Resource.** A comprehensive Web site that includes much valuable information itself and also has excellent links to other sites, along with listings of additional resources. (http://www.geocities.com/Athens/oracle/2469/welcome.html/)

**The Gardnerians.** This society consists of those who, as their Web site proclaims, have "crossed paths with John Gardner, or any of his work." They undertake extensive research into Gardner's life and career, including encouraging memoirs and recollections by colleagues and students of Gardner. (http://home.capu.net/gardnerians/)

**The John C. Gardner Appreciation Page.** This Web site is the source for a host of John Gardner resources, including information on the dates, times, and locations for seminars, conferences, and festivals related to Gardner and his writing. (http://www.sunygenesee.cc.ny.us/gardner/gardner.htm).

**The Thomas Fasano John Gardner Site.** This Web site is an eclectic mixture of articles, bibliographical citations, photographs, and other materials relating to the author and his writings. It also provides links to other Web sites of interest to students of John Gardner. (http://home1.gte.net/tomchat/gardner.htm).

*MICHAEL WITKOSKI*

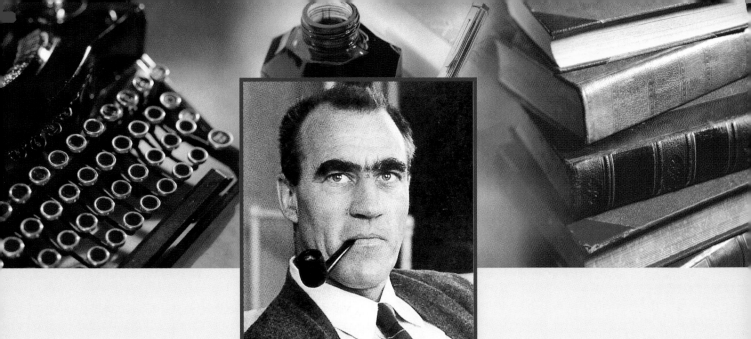

# William Gibson

**BORN:** November 13, 1914, New York, New York
**IDENTIFICATION:** Late-twentieth-century American dramatist best known for *The Miracle Worker* (1956), his play about Anne Sullivan and Helen Keller.

William Gibson has written dramatic and musical plays, nonfiction, and poetry. *The Miracle Worker*, his most well-known work, captures the intensely dramatic struggle between an isolated, frustrated child and her equally strong-willed teacher. Originally written for television, the play was soon adapted for the stage, where it has remained in production ever since. All of Gibson's works are marked by tender, humane regard for people in difficulty, realistic portrayals of strong-willed women, and the theme of language as a manifestation of the human urge to communicate and be understood.

William Gibson was born on November 13, 1914, to working-class parents in the Bronx area of New York City. His father, George Gibson, was an amateur piano player who worked for many years as a clerk in a bank. His Irish Catholic mother, Florence Gibson, came from a musical family. Gibson's parents encouraged him to pursue an education, and he graduated from high school at the age of sixteen. He had pursued writing for some years on his own and was published for the first time in a school newspaper.

He entered the City College of New York, where he showed talent in his literature classes, as well as in playing the piano and writing, but in not much else. He was encouraged by one of his English professors, Theodore Goodman, who urged him to try writing a novel. After approximately two years, however, Gibson dropped out of college. After college, he practiced acting with the Barter Theater in Virginia and wrote several unproduced plays.

**Career Firsts.** After his first marriage ended in divorce in 1940, he married Margaret Brenman, a psychoanalyst. She practiced in a Topeka, Kansas, children's clinic and helped support Gibson as he wrote, worked odd jobs, and played and taught piano. In 1943 the Topeka Civic Theater staged Gibson's first play

Gibson at a reading of one of his plays in Baltimore, Maryland, in 1977. Gibson, who wrote in obscurity for ten years before one of his plays was produced in 1943, has never really attained critical acclaim for his two highly successful plays, *The Miracle Worker* and *Two for the Seesaw*.

to be produced, a one-act titled *I Lay in Zion*. Another play in three acts about the young William Shakespeare, *A Cry of Players*, was first produced in Topeka in 1948. During this time, Gibson published his poetry in various magazines, and a collection of poems that appeared in *Poetry* magazine won him the Harriet Monroe Memorial Prize in 1945.

In 1950 Gibson attended a playwriting seminar held by the American playwright Clifford Odets. The two men became lifelong friends, until Odets's death in 1963, and Gibson would cite Odets's work as a major influence on his own.

Gibson's only novel, *The Cobweb*, was published in 1945 under the pseudonym William Mass. The story focuses on conflicts among the staff of a mental clinic. The novel proved to be successful; it sold well and was made into a film. The money that Gibson earned from the sale of the film rights enabled him and his wife to buy a large house in Stockbridge, Massachusetts, where Margaret found employment at a nearby institution.

**Family Life and Success.** In 1953 the couple's first child, Thomas, was born. He was followed in 1956 by their second, Daniel. The growing family's financial resources were strained. In that year, 1956, Gibson showed producer Arthur Penn a draft of a play based on the true story of the teacher Anne Sullivan and her blind and deaf student, Helen Keller. Penn suggested that the draft be finished as a play for television. The play was broadcast live in early 1957 on the television show *Playhouse 90* and enjoyed widespread acclaim. Gibson lengthened the teleplay for stage production, and in 1959, the stage version premiered on Broadway. Anne Bancroft played Anne, and Patty Duke played Helen. The play's technical accomplishment was widely hailed: Helen, the child, is blind and deaf, and can only express herself physically. In one noted scene, the child and teacher engage in a prolonged, eloquent conflict almost entirely devoid of words. The play was a success and ran for two years on Broadway. Duke and Bancroft also starred in the third version of the play, produced as a film

This photograph of Gibson, with his son on his shoulders, was taken in Stockbridge, Massachusetts, by local photographer Clemens Kalischer around 1960. Kalischer still remains in touch with Gibson.

in 1962. Gibson wrote the screenplay, which was nominated for an Academy Award.

**A Second Broadway Hit.** Gibson's next play, *Two for the Seesaw*, appeared on Broadway in 1958. The plot concerns the relationship between Jerry Ryan, a depressed lawyer whose wife in Omaha is in the process of divorcing him, and Gittel Mosca, a high-spirited Jewish ballerina from the Bronx. Bancroft played Gittel, and Henry Fonda played Jerry. In preparing this play for Broadway, Gibson had his first painful experience with multiple rewrites undertaken to increase the odds of audience approval. In his original version of *Two for the Seesaw*, Jerry's character was unsympathetic, and both Fonda and the producer, Penn, requested that he be made more likable.

Gibson recounts his rewriting travails in *The Seesaw Log: A Chronicle of the Stage Production, with the Text, of "Two for the Seesaw"* (1959).

In the case of *Two for the Seesaw*, the rewrites may have been beneficial, because the play was a success on Broadway, went on tour, and in 1962 was made into a film, the rights for which earned Gibson $600,000. In 1973 the play was produced as a musical, for which Michael Bennet wrote the spoken words, or in Broadway terms, the "book." In 1963, soon after the success of *Two for the Seesaw*, Gibson's friend and fellow dramatist Clifford Odets died, leaving the book for the Broadway musical version of his play *The Golden Boy* (1937) unfinished. Gibson completed the book, and the musical entitled *Golden Boy* had a successful Broadway run from 1964 to 1965.

**A Change in Direction.** In 1971 a bleeding ulcer, the same condition that had gravely affected both of his parents, almost claimed Gibson's life. His illness caused him to reassess his spiritual beliefs. On the example of his son, Thomas, he studied transcendental meditation. He also returned to the Roman Catholicism of his childhood, began attending Mass again, and wrote three liturgical dramas. The first, *The Body and the Wheel: A Play Made from the Gospels* (1974), retells the story of the Passion, the last days and resurrection of Christ. *The Butterfingers Angel, Mary and Joseph, Herod the Nut, and the Slaughter of Twelve Hit Carols in a Pear Tree* (1974) is a Christmas pageant featuring a clumsy angel and an outspoken, determined Mary. *Goodly Creatures* (1980) examines religious beliefs in seventeenth-century Massachusetts.

With *Golda* (1977), Gibson experienced one of his most draining failures. The play is about Golda Meir, the Israeli prime minister from 1969 to 1974. As he had with *Two for the Seesaw*, Gibson went through several rewrites at the behest of others. During this time Gibson often lived in a tent so that he would not be distracted from writing. Despite the efforts of all involved to make the play faultless, the critics were unforgiving when it opened on Broadway.

In 1982 Gibson wrote a sequel to *The Miracle Worker*, entitled *Monday after the Miracle*. The play, based on real events, examines Anne Sullivan's unsuccessful marriage years after the events of *The Miracle Worker*, when Helen Keller is a college student and Anne is her tutor.

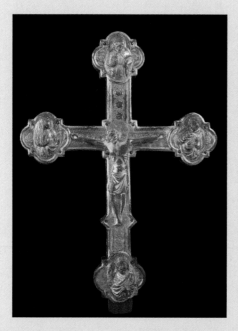 

Gibson approaches his religion both seriously and with a reverent sense of humor. The suffering of Christ, depicted in this Italian Renaissance crucifix, is portrayed in Gibson's liturgical drama *The Body and the Wheel*, while Gerrit Greve's 1996 image of an angel captures the lightheartedness of Gibson's *The Butterfingers Angel, Mary and Joseph, Herod the Nut, and the Slaughter of Twelve Hit Carols in a Pear Tree.*

# HIGHLIGHTS IN GIBSON'S LIFE

**1914**      William Gibson is born on November 13 in New York City.

**1930**      Graduates from high school.

**1930–1932** Attends City College of New York, is encouraged in writing by his professor, Theodore Goodman.

**1936–1939** Studies acting and writes unproduced plays.

**1940**      Moves to Topeka, Kansas; marries Margaret Brenman.

**1943**      His one-act play *I Lay in Zion* is produced in Topeka.

**1945**      Gibson wins Harriet Monroe Memorial Prize for a group of his poems published in *Poetry* magazine.

**1948**      His play about the young William Shakespeare, *A Cry of Players*, is produced in Topeka.

**1948**      Gibson publishes, *Winter Crook*, a book of poems.

**1950**      Attends a playwrights' seminar led by Clifford Odets and becomes Odets's lifelong friend.

**1953**      First son, Thomas, is born.

**1954**      Gibson publishes *The Cobweb*, a successful novel.

**1955**      Gibson writes screenplay for film version of *The Cobweb*.

**1956**      Second son, Daniel, is born in family's new home, Stockbridge, Massachusetts.

**1957**      Teleplay of *The Miracle Worker* premieres on live television.

**1958**      *Two for the Seesaw* begins a successful Broadway run.

**1959**      *The Miracle Worker*, revised for the stage, begins a successful run on Broadway.

**1962**      Film version of *The Miracle Worker*, for which Gibson wrote the screenplay, premieres.

**1962**      Film version of *Two for the Seesaw* premieres.

**1968**      Gibson publishes *A Mass for the Dead*, a memoir honoring his parents and other relatives.

**1971**      Nearly dies of a bleeding ulcer.

**1972**      Begins study of transcendental meditation; returns to the Roman Catholicism of his childhood.

**1974**      Liturgical play *The Body and the Wheel: A Play Made from the Gospels* is produced.

**1977**      *Golda*, a play about Golda Meir, flops on Broadway.

**1982**      *Monday after the Miracle*, another play about Anne Sullivan and Helen Keller, is produced.

**1984**      Presented with the William Inge Playwright Award for outstanding contributions to the American theater.

# The Writer's Work

William Gibson is best known for his Broadway plays *The Miracle Worker* (1959) and *Two for the Seesaw* (1958). In addition, he has written a novel, a book of poetry, and four memoirs. All of his works are marked by a tender, humane regard for people in difficulty. Gibson's realistic portrayals of strong-willed women are also noteworthy. Finally, an overriding theme of his work is language as the manifestation of the human urge to communicate and be understood. For much of his career, Gibson wrote for Broadway.

**Gibson and Broadway.** In the late 1950s a Broadway premiere was the highest mark of success in both serious drama and musical theater. Neither Gibson nor anyone else has ever simply arrived on Broadway without prior accomplishment. Gibson's long preparation for the success of *The Miracle Worker* may be traced back to his late teenage years, when, despite fears about his prospects, he resolved that, rather than complete college and then teach, he would become a writer. For approximately the next ten years, he lived in obscurity, often earning less than he needed to support himself, but wrote continuously. It was not until 1943, when Gibson was twenty-nine years old, that a play of his was produced—in Topeka, Kansas.

Gibson took another step toward Broadway after almost another decade with his novel, *The Cobweb* (1954), which sold well and was made into a film. Finally, in 1955, Gibson received the opportunity to write the book, the spoken words of a musical, for *The Ruby*, a one-act lyrical drama slated for Broadway. Gibson had begun to reach his stride.

**Common Characteristics.** Some examples of Gibson's playwriting traits can be found in *A Cry of Players*, which was first produced in Topeka in 1948 and later on Broadway. The play speculates on the young adulthood of

William Shakespeare, presenting him as faced with the difficult decision of whether to be a responsible tradesman who supports his wife and children or the inspired artist he feels destined to become. Will behaves badly toward his wife, yet is charming and sympathetic in his noble aspirations. His wife, Anne, also emerges as a highly sympathetic character. She engages in a physical fight with a rival for Will's affections and argues, forcefully and publicly, with the most powerful man in the village on Will's behalf.

In some of the play's best scenes, Anne endeavors to get through to Will, trying to convince him to take a job as a schoolteacher and to make him love her again. She tries every kind of language she can think of to reach him. She fails to get him to do what she wants, but she does not fail to reach him and therefore gains a measure of acceptance of her situation. In Gibson's plays, the urge to get through to another person, to persuade or gain understanding, is always a significant theme.

**Gibson's Masterpiece.** *The Miracle Worker* makes the best presentation of Gibson's characteristic themes. Anne Sullivan, the play's principal character, is often sharp-tongued and difficult, but Gibson reveals her humanity and suffering. She is haunted by her nightmarish childhood, which she has just begun to leave behind. With equal humaneness, he shows that although Helen can be an annoying, scheming brat, she is also pitiably frustrated at her inability to communicate. He also presents Captain Arthur Keller sympathetically—as a man who has been disappointed by too many unsuccessful attempted cures for his afflicted child—when a less empathetic writer could have portrayed Arthur as nothing more than the family autocrat.

Anne is a supreme example of Gibson's ability to portray strong women, and in this regard seven-year-old Helen is also quite memorable.

In the mid-1950s, Gibson came across a collection of Anne Sullivan's letters in a Stockbridge, Massachusetts, library. They detailed her experiences working with an impaired girl named Helen Keller. *The Miracle Worker,* shown here in a still from the 1962 film, starring Anne Bancroft as Anne Sullivan and Patty Duke as Helen Keller, was born.

What unites Helen and Anne is their fierce determination to communicate. Both are deeply isolated, even among people. Helen is isolated by her lack of language, and Anne by her painful self-consciousness and uncertain social status.

## Factual Bases for Gibson's Plays.

Among Gibson's works, *The Miracle Worker* is preeminent, but it has something unusual in common with his other works. Although many playwrights base their dramas on true stories, *The Miracle Worker*, *Golda*, *Monday after the Miracle*, and *John and Abigail* (1969) are all highly faithful to fact. Most playwrights use slivers of fact to support a house of speculation, as is the case with *A Cry of Players*.

However, most of Gibson's works are steeped in fact.

### BIBLIOGRAPHY

Bordman, Gerald. *The American Musical Theater*. New York: Oxford University Press, 1978.

Coy, Stephen C. "William Gibson." In *Dictionary of Literary Biography*. Vol. 7 in *Twentieth-Century American Dramatists*. Detroit: Gale Research, 1978.

Laufe, Abe. *Anatomy of a Hit*. New York: Hawthorn Books, 1966.

Mordden, Ethan. *The American Theatre*. New York: Oxford University Press, 1981.

Weales, Gerald Clifford. *American Drama Since World War II*. New York: Harcourt, Brace, 1962.

Wilmeth, Don B. *The Cambridge History of American Theatre*. New York: Cambridge University Press, 2000.

# Reader's Guide to Major Works

## THE MIRACLE WORKER

**Genre:** Drama
**Subgenre:** Psychological realism
**Produced:** New York, 1957
**Time period:** 1880s
**Setting:** Tuscumbia, Alabama

**Themes and Issues.** *The Miracle Worker* is about communication as the foundation of the human community. It illustrates how all people must struggle, and some heroically, to communicate and thus be part of that community. The play is unequivocally optimistic about the potential of human beings for change and growth. At the end of the play, the obstinate hope of the teacher, Anne Sullivan, that her deaf and blind student, Helen Keller, can communicate has triumphed. *The Miracle Worker* is a rarity in that it explores a common relationship that is underrepresented in theater: that of student and teacher. As the clash of wills and the ultimate bonding of Helen and Anne make clear, that relationship can be full of drama.

**The Plot.** Kate and Arthur Keller, who live in rural Alabama, face the growing problem of their young daughter, Helen, who has been deaf and blind since an illness in infancy. Out of misguided pity, the family has spoiled Helen to the extent that she has become dangerous. For example, she does not hesitate to pitch a baby out of its cradle so that she can use the cradle for her doll. Arthur refuses his wife's suggestions to consult yet another doctor.

Anne, played by Anne Bancroft, stands up to Helen, played by Patty Duke, during one of her dinnertime tantrums, in this scene from the 1959 Broadway production. Duke once called the scene "the heart of the play. . . . The battle lasts ten minutes onstage and although it scares the life out of you, it was intricately choreographed like a ballet . . . every single moment in the scene was written by William Gibson."

Nevertheless, faced with the prospect of either institutionalizing, chaining, or physically punishing Helen to keep her from assaulting others, Arthur agrees to make one more try to help his daughter.

The family recruits a young woman, Anne Sullivan, from Boston to tutor Helen. Anne is only twenty years old and a complete stranger, but the Kellers have some hope that she can reach their daughter. Anne, who has taught other blind children, immediately begins to teach Helen words by finger-spelling, or touching Helen's palm in various finger patterns, one pattern for each letter. Although Helen demonstrates her intelligence by learning words quickly, she does not grasp the connection between the words she is memorizing and the things they represent.

Anne's diligence with Helen has painful motivations. Whenever Anne is alone, she is haunted by her horrific childhood in a poorhouse, and, in particular, the loss of her younger brother, who had been her only family. Although she was powerless to prevent their separation by authorities, she still feels tremendous guilt over being unable to keep her promise to love him (and, the implication is clear, to protect him) forever.

In the meantime, Helen continues to behave like a savage, and the family is disappointed in Anne, who nevertheless is able to persuade Kate and Arthur to isolate Helen with her in a garden house for two weeks. Remarkably, in these two weeks Anne teaches Helen to behave. However, when Helen is returned to the family, she immediately reverts to her old be-

## PLAYS

1943    I Lay in Zion
1948    A Cry of Players
1948    Dinny and the Witches: A Frolic on Grave Matters
1957    The Miracle Worker (televised)
1958    Two for the Seesaw
1959    The Miracle Worker (staged)
1964    Golden Boy (musical adaptation of Clifford Odets's play, music by Charles Strouse, lyrics by Lee Adams)
1969    John and Abigail
1971    American Primitive (revision of John and Abigail)
1974    The Body and the Wheel: A Play Made from the Gospels
1974    The Butterfingers Angel, Mary and Joseph, Herod the Nut, and the Slaughter of Twelve Hit Carols in a Pear Tree

1977    Golda
1980    Goodly Creatures
1982    Monday after the Miracle
1984    Handy Dandy
1984    Raggedy Ann and Andy (also as Rag Dolly and Raggedy Ann; music and lyrics by Joe Raposo)

## SCREENPLAYS

1957    The Cobweb (under pseudonym William Mass)
1962    The Miracle Worker

## LONG FICTION

1954    The Cobweb (under pseudonym William Mass)

## POETRY

1948    Winter Crook

## NONFICTION

1959    The Seesaw Log: A Chronicle of the Stage Production, with the Text, of "Two for the Seesaw"
1968    A Mass for the Dead
1974    A Season in Heaven
1978    Notes on How to Turn a Phoenix into Ashes: The Story of the Stage Production, with the Text, of "Golda"
1978    Shakespeare's Game

haviors. In the ensuing physical struggle, Helen empties a pitcher of water on Anne, who angrily picks the child up to take her outside to the water pump to refill the pitcher. Even at this moment, however, when Anne is aware that she may be fired and all her efforts may be wasted, she remembers to finger-spell "water" into Helen's palm as water runs over it.

At that moment, the miracle worker, who is Anne, works her miracle, which is the awakening of Helen through language. Helen recognizes the connection between the word *water* spelled onto her palm and the water. Ecstatic, the girl rushes about the front yard, demanding to learn the names of what she touches: "ground," "step," "trellis," "mother," "papa," and finally "teacher," or Anne. Helen embraces

Anne, and Anne gives Helen the same promise that she gave her brother: "I love Helen, forever and ever."

**Analysis.** *The Miracle Worker* is significant in its close adherence to historical fact. Events depicted in the play, although condensed for dramatic effect, generally happened as they are depicted. This dedication to realism helps temper the play's melodrama. *The Miracle Worker*, after all, is about a young orphaned woman and a little girl who is blind and deaf. To add to the risk of emotional excess, the two struggle furiously at the beginning of the play and embrace at the end, with Anne consciously giving Helen the same promise that she gave to her dead brother. The play's strong context of

## SOME INSPIRATIONS BEHIND GIBSON'S WORK

Gibson has noted that his primary motivation as a writer is a standard one: He enjoys working with pen and paper and words on a page, and he has never been much good at anything else. In his youth, he discovered another common reason for his desire to write. He wished to avoid his parents' fate. In his eyes, their daily toil as a clerk and a cleaning woman provided them with food and shelter, but at the price of their spirit. He resolved to risk poverty to do what he enjoyed.

Writers seldom develop without the encouragement of mentors, and Gibson had two. The first was Theodore Goodman, who taught writing at the City College of New York, where Gibson was a student. Goodman encouraged Gibson's creative ambitions and urged him to write long fiction. The second was playwright Clifford Odets. In 1950, when Gibson was an up-and-coming playwright, he attended a seminar led by Odets, who at the time was famous for such dramas as *The Golden Boy* (1937). The two became lifelong friends.

Finally, in the early 1970s, a serious illness and an encounter with the benefits of transcendental meditation inspired Gibson to return to the Roman Catholicism of his childhood and to write three religiously inspired plays. Even into the early 1980s, after approximately thirty years of professional writing, Gibson's work was still produced on Broadway.

A friend and colleague of Gibson's, Clifford Odets started out as an actor, but quickly turned his attention to playwriting. He is considered to be among the most gifted of the American social-protest dramatists of the 1930s.

details of time and place, helped to make it a masterpiece. However, although it ranks as one of the most accomplished American dramas of the twentieth century, it has been largely ignored by critics.

Heroic, strong-willed women characters are a staple of Gibson's plays, and Anne is a prime example. She is outspoken almost to the point of being self-defeating, fully aware of her own pain and insecurity. Ultimately though she is hard to browbeat. Other strong Gibson women include Anne, William Shakespeare's wife in *A Cry of Players*; Golda in *Golda*; Mary in *The Butterfingers Angel, Herod the Nut, and the Slaughter of Twelve Hit Carols in a Pear Tree*; and Gittel in *Two for the Seesaw*.

## SOURCES FOR FURTHER STUDY

Laufe, Abe. *Anatomy of a Hit*. New York: Hawthorn Books, 1966.

Mordden, Ethan. *The American Theatre*. New York: Oxford University Press, 1981.

Wilmeth, Don B. *The Cambridge History of American Theatre*. New York: Cambridge University Press, 2000.

## TWO FOR THE SEESAW

**Genre:** Drama
**Subgenre:** Psychological realism
**Produced:** New York, 1958
**Time period:** 1950s
**Setting:** New York City

**Themes and Issues.** Gibson's most prevalent theme—that humans need to communicate and that communication humanizes—is strongly evident in this play, in which a man and a woman meet, have a relationship, and

A scene from Gibson's 1958 theatrical success, *Two for the Seesaw*. Anne Bancroft again starred, this time as Gittel, the strong, yet fragile ballerina who is afraid of intimacy. Henry Fonda appeared as Jerry, a man dissatisfied with his life of luxury, handed to him at the cost of his own independence.

part. They are the only two characters in the play, which is about almost nothing but their relationship. In concentrating in detail on one relationship in New York City in the 1950s, Gibson is able to provide insight into all romantic relationships.

The man is Jerry Ryan, a conventional lawyer who has just moved to New York from Nebraska. The woman is Gittel Mosca, an eccentric Jewish New Yorker. Their relationship is initially tentative and hesitant. Jerry is depressed and seeks emotional solace from Gittel. At the same time, he is wary of emotional involvement because he is still hurting from his separation from his wife. As he puts it when making his first date with Gittel, "Once you break your leg in five places you hesitate to step out." Gittel, who does not always follow the lawyer's verbal turns, mistakenly takes this literally. From the beginning, however, she is unerring in her emotional understanding of him. She sees, for example, that Jerry wants to treat her as a kind of emotional salve, but she also sees that he has some potential to meet her needs. She is alone, after all, and Jerry is at least willing to engage in honest conversation with her, even if, especially at first, his conversation is heavily larded with defensive banter.

Jerry needs Gittel, and she needs him. They find themselves compelled not only to talk to each other but also to get through to each other. As the play's title indicates, they engage in a balancing act of defensiveness and vulnerability. Their conversations rise and fall on declarations of need and willingness or the lack thereof. The title also makes clear that a seesaw—like a relationship—needs two to work. There is no exchange, no negotiation, without another person.

The play focuses intently on the details of setting—such as small New York apartments, a discussion on the merits of an icebox instead of a refrigerator, and the use of an operator to make long-distance calls—to provide a realistic context to what might otherwise be a generalized discussion of how men and women begin, conduct, and end romantic relationships. Nevertheless, in concentrating on these telling details, Gibson encompasses universal truths about men and women.

**The Plot.** Jerry obtains Gittel's phone number at a party and calls her later, ostensibly about his interest in buying her icebox. After a considerable but realistic amount of verbal back-and-forth, he asks her on a date, and she accepts.

The two nearly sleep together on their first date. Jerry is seductive but hesitant; Gittel tries to get him to be more emotionally forthright. As their emotional card game continues, mostly over the telephone, their personal histories unfold. Gittel, at thirty, suffers from an ulcer and is aging out of her less-than-stellar career in dance. Jerry, a lawyer from Nebraska, is deeply depressed and has left home because his wife has left him for another man. He regrets taking so many handouts from his father-in-law, and yet, as Gittel points out to him, he is asking her for favor after favor.

Jerry and Gittel become lovers, and he becomes more open and sincere in his regard for her. They establish more connections. Jerry buys Gittel a loft so that she can increase her faltering income as a costume maker and dance teacher, and he begins to look for ways to practice law in New York. He discovers, however, that his wife is rethinking their separation. The telephone that connects Jerry to Gittel and a new life in New York also connects him to Nebraska and his very recently severed ties there. Ironically, Gittel has helped him prepare to be emotionally open enough to forgive his wife and admit to himself that he still loves her. Ultimately, he decides to return to his wife. Although Gittel loses Jerry, she is not defeated. Rather, she is affirmative, saying to him as they part: "Long as you *live* I want you to remember the last thing you heard out of me was I love you." Jerry, at last, is worthy of her love. Rather than make a wisecrack, he says simply, "I love you too, Gittel," before going back to Omaha.

**Analysis.** The play's most innovative feature is its use of the stage. On one side of the stage is Jerry's cheap room, and on the other is Gittel's messy apartment in another part of town. When the two talk to each other on the telephone, the audience hears both sides of the conversation. They are the only two characters in the play, but when they are not talking to each other they are often on the phone with others. Gibson's technical achievement is in making these phone calls, of which the audience hears only one side, both comprehensible and dramatically relevant. Gibson also makes adroit use of the set; in one scene, for example (decades before call waiting), the two grow increasingly frustrated as they alternate calling each other, each time getting a busy signal while the other fields other calls. In the end,

Nick Cudworth's 2000 oil painting *Long-Distance Information* conveys the timeless need to communicate, a prevailing issue in Gibson's work. The telephone becomes a potent symbol of emotional distance and connection in *Two for the Seesaw.*

Gittel gets through to Jerry but is so frustrated that she tells him only that their next date is canceled. In this play, Gibson's central topic—the human desire to get through to another person—is presented quite literally.

Gittel is more exuberant and likable than Jerry, and thus it is easy to mistakenly believe that he is the only one who benefits from their relationship. He honestly tells her, however, that she is too trusting, too easily victimized, and too likely to confuse wishful thinking with reality. It is ironic that nearly any advice columnist or therapist would tell Gittel that it is someone precisely like Jerry, a married man, who is likely to take advantage of those traits he warns her about. Married men, the trusted adviser would say, always go back to their wives, and that is what Jerry does. At the end of the play, however, Gittel is not Jerry's victim. She has entered into the relationship with her eyes open, and he has helped to open them.

As is the case with his *The Miracle Worker*, Gibson's *Two for the Seesaw* has suffered critical neglect, presumably because of its unabashed, but defensible, sentimentality. On the other hand, imitation is better praise than analysis, and the character of Gittel Mosca—ditsy yet incisive, sharp tongued, empathetic, and quick to fall for a handsome man—was widely imitated in subsequent films and Broadway plays. Various characters played by Barbra Streisand, for example, probably owe something to Gibson's Gittel.

## SOURCES FOR FURTHER STUDY

Coy, Stephen C. "William Gibson." In *Dictionary of Literary Biography*. Vol. 7 in *Twentieth-Century American Dramatists*. Detroit: Gale Research, 1978.

Gibson, William. *The Seesaw Log: A Chronicle of the Stage Production, with the Text, of "Two for the Seesaw."* New York: Knopf, 1959.

# Other Works

**A MASS FOR THE DEAD** (1968). This book is a plea for forgiveness for the sins that children inevitably commit against their parents, in particular Gibson's unremarkable sins against his own parents. A memoir about his mother and father, the book is arranged according to the parts of the Roman Catholic Mass. The narrative, however, is more chronological than thematic. The most moving portions detail, with direct simplicity, the working-class heroism and long, distressing final illnesses of his parents. Richly humane but confusingly vague on such facts as specific dates, names, and sequences of events, the book preserves the memory of the generation that went before Gibson and makes amends for the past.

Gibson's descriptions of his father's long final illness, which began with a bleeding ulcer, are especially harrowing and presented with great tenderness. Echoes of this family memory can be found in the illness of Gittel Mosca in *Two for the Seesaw*, and no doubt helps explain why Gibson's near-death from a bleeding ulcer in 1971 so deeply affected his life.

**GOLDA** (1977). The story of Golda Meir, Israel's prime minister from 1969 to 1974, seems like a perfect subject for a Broadway play. Any playwright who writes about her,

*Between the Wars #3*, a 1998 oil painting by Kathryn Jacobi, depicts an older couple standing on a platform at a train station but not preparing to go anywhere. Gibson felt that the constant toil of his parents forced them to sacrifice their personal freedom and development. For Gibson, writing was not only an escape but a means to a brighter future. His 1968 *A Mass for the Dead*, a memoir about his parents, is his love story to them.

Israeli Prime Minister Golda Meir is shown speaking at a press conference in Strasbourg, France, on October 2, 1973. Gibson, unique among male playwrights of his generation, often chose to write about strong central female characters. Although Gibson's play about Meir was hardly a success, it did help raise awareness about the accomplishments of this important leader.

however, is faced with some intractable problems, some of which arise from modern documentation. Many people know what Meir looked and sounded like. In addition, there is no shortage of factual information about her life and accomplishments. Any play, therefore, that attempts to dramatize her life is bound to strike a discordant note between fact and dramatization. *The Miracle Worker*, in contrast, portrays real events and people, but neither the people nor the events were widely known, and, not surprisingly, the play's version of events has not been dismissed as oversimplified. With *Golda*, however, Gibson was not so lucky. In *Notes on How to Turn a Phoenix into Ashes: The Story of the Stage Production, with the Text, of "Golda,"* Gibson recounts that, when he personally read the play aloud to Meir, she remarked, "I'm listening like it's somebody else."

The play focuses on the crisis of the Yom Kippur War of 1973, when Egypt and Syria in-

vaded Israel. Meir is surrounded by various generals and officials as she deals with this grave national threat. However, the play's accuracy in historical detail leads to such dramatically weak moments as the one in which Meir uses a telephone to ask a U.S. official for forty-eight Phantom jets. Onstage, this act is hard to distinguish from that of someone ordering a pizza.

*Golda* is moving, however, in its presentation of an indefatigable leader who can guide people out of even the most desperate crisis. For example, in a speech to the people of Israel, Meir's language is stirring and believable: "Citizens of Israel. Ordeal by battle has been forced on us again. Shortly before 2:00 P.M. today the armies of Egypt and Syria launched a series of attacks. . . . The Israeli defense forces have entered the fight." In private, she tells an aide to go home to sleep, saying, "I'm sleeping here on the couch, and for two there isn't room." Before entering politics, Meir was an émigré Russian schoolteacher who went from Milwaukee to Palestine in 1921. Ironically, it does not matter whether she actually spoke English such as "for two there isn't room"; such language reminds an American audience more of stand-up comedy than statesmanship.

The play has many strengths, but, as a final blow, Anne Bancroft, who played Golda, became too ill to perform shortly after the play opened, ending its short run.

## THE BUTTERFINGERS ANGEL, MARY AND JOSEPH, HEROD THE NUT, AND THE SLAUGHTER OF TWELVE HIT CAROLS IN A PEAR TREE (1974).

The play is a Christmas pageant that retells the story of Mary and Joseph in a funny but reverent way. In the play's version of events, Joseph is an older man in love with a young, tart-tongued, and head-strong Mary, who rejects him until she realizes that the baby she is carrying will need a good home, at which point she audaciously moves in with him. As the well-known story proceeds to its conclusion in the manger, other details are changed. This amiable, exuberant play includes many songs and succeeds in its aim of putting a fresh spin on the story of the birth of Jesus.

Other characters include the angel of the title, who occasionally drops the various objects, such as a book and a trumpet, that his office requires him to hold; a group of inarticulate louts, true to Gibson's recurring theme that lack of language equals savagery, who go around threatening violence; and various ordinary people who provide commentary on the main events of the play.

# Resources

The drama of William Gibson has been strangely neglected by scholars. Although *The Miracle Worker* continues to be widely produced, and the play *Two for the Seesaw* has been widely imitated, Gibson's dramatic art has not received much critical attention. Sources of interest for students of Gibson include the following:

**Berkshire Theatre Festival.** William Gibson was instrumental in supporting the Berkshire Theatre Festival, which takes place yearly in Stockbridge, Massachusetts. His play about the young William Shakespeare, *A Cry of Players*, was produced there in 1968, twenty years after its first production in Topeka, Kansas. (http://www.berkshiretheatre.org/)

**Ivy Green, Birthplace of Helen Keller.** Ivy Green, the cottage in Tuscumbia, Alabama, in which Helen Keller was born, is now a permanent shrine on the National Register of Historic Places. Every year, *The Miracle Worker* is performed on the grounds of the estate. (http://www.bham.net/keller/home.html)

**Anne Sullivan's Writings.** Excerpts from Anne Sullivan's *The Story of My Life*, in which she discusses the education of Helen Keller, are available on line. (http://digital.library.upenn.edu/women/keller/life/part-III.html)

ERIC HOWARD

# Nikki Giovanni

**BORN:** June 7, 1943, Knoxville, Tennessee

**IDENTIFICATION:** Late-twentieth-century poet, activist, essayist, academic, and lecturer, best known for her radical identification with the Civil Rights and Black Power movements in the 1960s as well as for her later works lauding black pride and the search for individual identity.

Nikki Giovanni's work serves as an inspiration for young, talented, ambitious blacks who seek a sense of ethnic identity or aspire to the arts. One of the most widely read and anthologized living poets, she was a forerunner of the black artistic renaissance of the 1960s and 1970s and a leader in the black oral poetry movement. Giovanni has a reputation for instilling a sense of racial pride in those she teaches and lectures. The author of multiple collections of poetry and various books of essays, she crosses the boundaries of ethnicity and age to touch the souls of multiple generations. She has received numerous accolades, including an honorary doctorate from, among others, Wilberforce University, the oldest black institution of higher learning in the United States.

# The Writer's Life

Yolande Cornelia Giovanni, Jr., later nick-named Nikki, was born in Knoxville, Tennessee, on June 7, 1943. At the time of her birth, Knoxville was a sleepy rural town with the ambition to urbanize. Her parents, Jones "Gus" Giovanni and Yolande Cornelia Watson Giovanni, were social workers who met while attending Knoxville College. In August of 1943 the Giovannis and their two daughters moved to Wyoming, Ohio, a suburb of Cincinnati, where Yolande took a position as supervisor of the Welfare Department.

Giovanni's maternal grandmother, Louvenia Terrell Watson, had the strongest impact on Giovanni's life. The two shared a deep connection, which in 1957 drew Giovanni back to Knoxville, Tennessee, where she lived with her grandparents while attending Austin High School during her sophomore and junior years. Both of her maternal grandparents gave her a strong sense of southern roots and respect for racial heritage. From her grandmother Giovanni learned the importance of deep familial connections and acquired a strong skepticism of whites, both characteristics which would thematically permeate her future work.

Charles White's 1974 painting *Mother Courage* echoes the spirit of Giovanni's maternal grandmother, Louvenia Terrell Watson, who first encouraged the poet to question the white-dominated world in which she was raised. She also provided her with her first model of a strong black woman, an image that would shape Giovanni's thinking and influence her writing throughout her career.

**College Years.** In 1960 Giovanni enrolled at Fisk University in Nashville, Tennessee, as an early entrant; however, her stay was abbreviated. After hearing of her grandfather's illness, she left campus to travel to Knoxville without seeking permission from the dean. Shortly after returning to Fisk, she was suspended from the university for displaying an attitude unbefitting a Fisk woman.

In 1961 her grandfather died, and Giovanni returned to her family in Ohio. There she worked as a cashier at a Walgreen's pharmacy and took occasional classes at the University of Cincinnati. Never one to accept rejection, however, she reenrolled at Fisk and returned to Nashville in 1964. Giovanni's college years in the 1960s took place during one

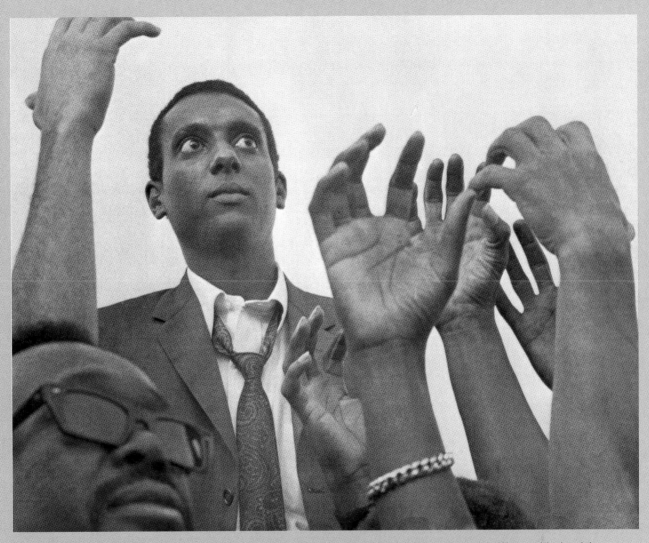

In this 1966 photograph, activist Stokely Carmichael addresses a crowd from the flatbed of a truck in Watts, a black neighborhood in Los Angeles, California, that suffered severe racial violence in 1965. Carmichael urged the citizens to become self-sufficient by forming their own city complete with its own police force and school system.

of the most turbulent eras in U.S. history, particularly for the young and for minorities. It was in this period that Giovanni found her milieu and the work that would direct the first phase of her life.

In response to her grandmother's teachings and to the growing unrest among college students and politically astute blacks, Giovanni was drawn to the Black Power movement, led by Stokely Carmichael of the Student Nonviolent Coordinating Committee (SNCC) and others. In 1965 Giovanni aided in the reestablishment of the SNCC at Fisk. Through that association and her penchant for the written word, she took root and grew in the polit-

ical soil surrounding the movements toward equality. She had always been an imaginative, intellectual, and inveterate reader, and at Fisk she discovered the topic for her later body of work, an audience for that work, and notoriety as an activist. In 1967 Giovanni graduated from Fisk University magna cum laude with a bachelor of arts degree in history.

Returning briefly to Ohio, Giovanni organized the first Cincinnati Black Arts Festival during the summer and enrolled at the University of Pennsylvania's School of Social Work with a Ford Foundation Fellowship. Although she decided that social work was not for her, the money enabled her to invest time in the creative process. Everything changed, however, after the 1968 assassination of Dr. Martin Luther King, Jr., the premier advocate of nonviolent protest during the Civil Rights movement. That tragedy served as the theme for some of the best reflective pieces of her early period.

**The Poet's Genesis.** Giovanni moved to New York in 1968 to attend Columbia University School of Fine Arts on a grant from the National Foundation of the Arts. She hoped to earn a master's degree in creative writing but withdrew from the program when her work was judged by conservative professors to be of little value. By the end of the year, she had borrowed money to publish her first volume of verse. *Black Feeling, Black Talk* (1968) garnered mixed reviews. One selection in particular, "Nigger/Can You Kill?," became the banner for the Civil Rights movement and infuriated many critics. In 1968 Giovanni published her second volume, *Black Judgement*, with a grant from the Harlem Council of the Arts. The impact of this work was immediate, and she was thrust into the center of the avant-garde literary arena.

In essence the year 1969 marked the second phase of Giovanni's life. She had decided against marriage early in life but now made the conscious choice to become a single mother. Her son, Thomas Watson Giovanni, was born on August 31, 1969, and quickly became the center of Giovanni's universe as well as a pervasive influence on the direction of her work. After his birth, she accepted academic appointments at Queens College of City University in New York, where she taught black history, and at Livingston College of Rutgers University, specializing in creative writing.

**Writer as Publisher.** In 1970 Giovanni founded her own publishing company, NikTom, Ltd., initially collecting poetry by black women, such as Gwendolyn Brooks and Margaret Walker. The edited volume *Night Comes Softly: Anthology of Black Female Voices* (1970) successfully launched the firm and afforded a reissue of her first two books as a combined volume as well as the publication of a third work, *Re: Creation* (1970).

Giovanni viewed poetry and music as inextricably linked, and in 1971 she proved that connection through the release of an album, *Truth Is on Its Way*. The recording featured spo-

Independent and outspoken, Giovanni's talents drew the attention of a wide audience. Here she is seen performing in the "Soul at the Center" series with the New York Community Choir at Lincoln Center in New York City on July 25, 1972. Giovanni appears in the bottom right corner. On the circuit again, Giovanni takes a break from her rehearsal for "Echoes and Silences," also at Lincoln Center, on June 21, 1973 (right).

# HIGHLIGHTS IN GIOVANNI'S LIFE

**1943**   Yolande Cornelia Giovanni, Jr., is born on June 7 in Knoxville, Tennessee; moves with family to Ohio.

**1960**   Enters Fisk University in Nashville, Tennessee.

**1961**   Dismissed from Fisk for leaving campus without permission.

**1964**   Reenters Fisk.

**1965**   Reestablishes Student Nonviolent Coordinating Committee at Fisk.

**1967**   Graduates from Fisk with honors; enters graduate program at University of Pennsylvania.

**1968**   Attends funeral of Dr. Martin Luther King, Jr.; moves to New York City; publishes *Black Feeling, Black Talk* and *Black Judgement*.

**1969**   Son, Thomas, is born; Giovanni teaches at Queens College and Rutgers University.

**1970**   Founds NikTom, Ltd., her own publishing company.

**1971**   Records *Truth Is on Its Way*; publishes *Gemini: An Extended Autobiographical Statement on My First Twenty-five Years of Being a Black Poet* and *Spin A Soft Black Song: Poems for Children.*

**1972**   Joins lecture circuit; publishes *My House.*

**1973**   Named Woman of the Year by *Ladies' Home Journal*; tours Africa for U.S. State Department; publishes *A Dialogue: James Baldwin and Nikki Giovanni.*

**1974**   Receives honorary doctorate from Wilberforce University.

**1975**   Publishes *The Women and the Men.*

**1978**   Publishes *Cotton Candy on a Rainy Day*; moves to Cincinnati to care for father.

**1984**   Appointed visiting professor at Ohio State University; receives death threats for her opposition to South African boycott.

**1985**   Named to Ohio Women's Hall of Fame; named Outstanding Woman of Tennessee; goes on European lecture tour.

**1989**   Accepts permanent position as professor of English at Virginia Polytechnic Institute.

ken poetry against a variation of musical backgrounds, primarily gospel and rhythmic beats. The album was among the top best-sellers of that year and generated three others to follow, one of which, *Truth*, received the AFTRA Award for the best spoken album of the year in 1972.

## The Lecture Circuit.

The decade of the 1970s marked the peak of Giovanni's popularity as a lecturer, and she spoke to approximately two hundred audiences annually, primarily on college campuses. Praised as a symbol of black awareness, Giovanni's constant appearance on the lecture circuit garnered recognition and economic rewards. In 1972 her standard fee for a university appearance was two thousand dollars per day. In 1973 the scope of her lectures widened as she visited Africa, sponsored by the U.S. State Department. This trip provided her with images for her work over the next few years and changed the course of her writing as she realized the universality of people and conditions.

Subsequent years brought Giovanni a stylistic mellowing; further publishing ventures; numerous awards, including at least seven honorary doctorates; and positions at a variety of universities. She ultimately settled at Virginia Polytechnic University in Blacksburg, Virginia, as a professor of English in 1989.

In Radcliffe Bailey's 1998 painting *Roots that Never Die,* family and a strong sense of origins are of central importance. "My Southern roots come out because of my sense of remembrance," Giovanni once said in an interview.

# The Writer's Work

Dubbed the "Princess of Black Poetry," Nikki Giovanni is best known for her radical activist work during the Civil Rights movement of the 1960s. Her later offerings, which include essays and spoken-word recordings, met with greater critical acclaim. In spite of attempts by critics to classify Giovanni as a revolutionary, a feminist, or a southerner, she evolved in her art as a direct result of personal rites of passage.

Giovanni's work is of an intensely personal nature, marking the intersection between life and art and reflecting the phases of her individual self-discovery as an African American, as a woman, and as a poet. Her poetry tears at many of the classic stereotypes associated with those roles, speaking for all with a cross-generational, multi-ethnic voice. Although she claims to speak for no one but herself, she is a poet of the people and a voice for many diverse groups.

**The Black Voice.** Giovanni has consistently adopted the role of spokesperson for black pride. Her initial volumes, which reflected the violence of the 1960s and the militarism of the Black Power movement, introduced a new style in black poetry: free verse expounded by an urban voice, offering blackness as a theme, both personal and communal. Combining private and public concerns, the poetry commands African Americans, particularly the young, to seize control of their own destinies. Giovanni's early work is lyrical, insistent, and often labeled as "hate poetry." The writing from her more introspective middle period indicates a sense of frustration, futility, and boredom with the advances—or lack thereof—of movements toward equality. Her later works are more reflective and reveal a mature outlook of hopefulness.

Looking the part of professor, Giovanni was photographed in 2000 in front of a chalkboard during a lesson at Virginia Polytechnic Institute in Blacksburg, Virginia, where she accepted a permanent teaching position in 1989.

# SOME INSPIRATIONS BEHIND GIOVANNI'S WORK

The major influence in Nikki Giovanni's life and work was her grandmother, Louvenia Terrell Watson. As a pioneering and outspoken member of the National Association for the Advancement of Colored People (NAACP), Watson was forced to leave Georgia and move to Tennessee. She instilled in her granddaughter a sense of pride in both her southern and her African American roots. The majority of Giovanni's activist spirit, Black Power poetry, and early antiwhite sentiment is directly attributable to her grandmother's tutelage.

The decade of the 1960s inspired many young people of the era to fight, both for their country and for their beliefs, while advocating peace and love. The inherent contradictions in fighting for peace and justice had a profound influence on Giovanni. Aligned with the Black Power movement, she became a spokesperson for the rights of blacks and a poet of the revolution.

Giovanni's lecture tours to the Caribbean and Africa in 1973 broadened her view of the world and altered her perspective on black civil rights. She realized that racial oppression was not native to the United States but universal in scope. As Giovanni adopted a more humanistic worldview following these excursions, her poems become more richly textured than many that had come before.

Another inspirational beacon for Giovanni was the birth of her son, Thomas, in 1969, which ushered in new motivation for success and a new audience for her work. She accepted positions on university faculties; founded a publishing company, NikTom, Ltd.; and wrote several books of poetry for children.

**Sense of Place.** Another facet of Giovanni's poetry is that of a clearly defined sense of place, whether that place is outward and concerned with social issues or inward with a focus on family, relationships, and the home. In some selections, Giovanni's outlook is more global, influenced in part by her visits to the Caribbean and Africa, which universalized her concept of the black struggle for equality. Giovanni attempts to see herself and others in relation to their place in the universe. Family, whether one's own family or the family of humankind, is always at the core of her work. It parallels the delineation of place, defines a search for identity, and illustrates the theme of belonging through a deep connection with the past. As for many black writers, that past is for Giovanni connected to African roots, and Africa is the setting for many of her poems.

Overall, there is an autobiographical thread woven through the body of her work, with Giovanni herself as the protagonist of each narrative.

**Use of Language.** Stylistically, Giovanni creates in a telegraphic mode, using clear and concise word selection, short staccato phrases, rhythmic repetition, and vernacular imagery. Primarily written in monologues, her work reflects her belief that black speech, black music, and black poetry are inseparable. That intermingling is revealed as she moves effortlessly between the idiom of the cultured urbanite to the speech patterns of the street.

**Literary Legacy.** Giovanni will be read for generations as representative of the black voice of the 1960s. Her work transcends that period of unrest, however, and has come to represent many areas of the African American experience, including musical association, family loyalty, and the search for identity. Always controversial, Giovanni remains a role model for young African Americans who seek self-discovery through the arts and a connection with their past.

## BIBLIOGRAPHY

Fowler, Virginia C. *Nikki Giovanni*. New York: Twayne Publishers, 1992.

Gibson, Donald B., ed. *Modern Black Poets: A Collection of Critical Essays*. Englewood Cliffs, N.J.: Prentice-Hall, 1973.

Henderson, Stephen. *Understanding the New Black Poetry: Black Speech and Black Music as Poetic References*. New York: William Morrow, 1973.

Lee, Don L. *Dynamic Voices I: Black Poets of the 1960s*. Detroit: Broadside Press, 1971.

Major, Clarence. *The Dark and the Feeling: Black Writers and Their Work*. New York: Third Press, 1974.

Mazer, Gwen. "Lifestyle: Nikki Giovanni." *Harper's Bazaar*, July 1972, 50–51.

Noble, Jean. *Beautiful, Also, Are the Souls of My Black Sisters: A History of the Black Woman in America*. Englewood Cliffs, N.J.: Prentice-Hall, 1978.

Palmer, R. Roderick. "The Poetry of Three Revolutionists: Don L. Lee, Sonia Sanchez, and Nikki Giovanni." *College Language Association Journal* 15 (September 1971): 25–36.

Robinson, Anna T. *Nikki Giovanni: From Revolution to Revelation*. Columbus: State Library of Ohio, 1979.

## POETRY

| 1968 | Black Feeling, Black Talk |
| 1968 | Black Judgement |
| 1970 | Black Feeling, Black Talk/Black Judgement |
| 1970 | Re: Creation |
| 1970 | Poem of Angela Yvonne Davis |
| 1972 | My House |
| 1975 | The Women and the Men |
| 1978 | Cotton Candy on a Rainy Day |
| 1983 | Those Who Ride the Night Winds |
| 1996 | Selected Poems of Nikki Giovanni |
| 1996 | The Genie in the Jar |
| 1996 | The Sun Is So Quiet: Poems |
| 1997 | Love Poems |
| 1999 | Blues: For All the Changes: New Poems |

## NONFICTION

| 1971 | Gemini: An Extended Autobiographical Statement on My First Twenty-five Years of Being a Black Poet |
| 1973 | A Dialogue: James Baldwin and Nikki Giovanni |
| 1974 | A Poetic Equation: Conversations Between Nikki Giovanni and Margaret Walker |
| 1988 | Sacred Cows . . . and Other Edibles |
| 1994 | Racism 101 |

## CHILDREN'S LITERATURE

| 1971 | Spin a Soft Black Song: Poems for Children |
| 1973 | Ego-Tripping and Other Poems for Young Readers |
| 1980 | Vacation Time: Poems for Children |
| 1994 | Knoxville, Tennessee |

## EDITED TEXTS

| 1970 | Night Comes Softly: Anthology of Black Female Voices |
| 1991 | Appalachian Elders: A Warm Hearth Sampler (with Cathee Dennison) |
| 1994 | Grand Mothers: Poems, Reminiscences, and Short Stories about the Keepers of Our Traditions |
| 1996 | Shimmy Shimmy Shimmy Like My Sister Kate: Looking at the Harlem Renaissance through Poems |
| 1999 | Grand Fathers: Reminiscences, Poems, Recipes, and Photos of the Keepers of Our Traditions |

## BLACK FEELING, BLACK TALK/BLACK JUDGEMENT

**Genre:** Poetry
**Subgenre:** Social protest
**Published:** New York, 1970
**Time period:** 1960s
**Setting:** United States

**Themes and Issues.** This volume, a combined version of Nikki Giovanni's two earliest and privately published collections, established her radical reputation. As a product of a historical moment frozen in time, this collection of poems can be viewed as representative of the racial unrest in the United States during the 1960s. Inspired by the Black Power movement, the poems of *Black Feeling, Black Talk*, privately published in 1968, issued such a piercing cry for revolutionary change that it sold two thousand copies that year.

The second section, *Black Judgement*, privately published later in 1968, takes a more militant tone and reflects the period in which heroes—John F. Kennedy, Robert Kennedy, Dr. Martin Luther King, Jr., and Malcolm X—were being assassinated with seeming regularity. These poems address alienation and displacement with a sense of rage against whites. With the release of these works, Giovanni was branded a radical and many of the critics labeled the collection "hate poetry."

**The Poems.** The free-verse poems of these collections are rich, complex, and emotionally demanding. Giovanni veers away from the traditional rural southern dialect previously employed in much African American poetry and speaks in a radically new poetic idiom using the diction and phrasing of contemporary urban black English. The militant tone of many of the poems belies their complex intellectual texture. Even the poem that is most often viewed as a call to revolution, "Nigger/Can You Kill?," changes mood through close reading. If

one examines the rhetoric closely, it seems that Giovanni is asking whether African Americans can really commit to murder for the cause, implying that dying for a cause is perhaps easier than killing for one. Another underlying assumption in the poem is that negative, pejorative aspects of language have kept blacks subjugated. Giovanni calls for the abolition of such destructive terms.

Another of the more radical, political poems, "The Great Pax Whitie," exhibits Giovanni's stylistic strengths. Depicting history as a linear progression of oppression of one race by another, the poem illustrates violence in the United States but offers no solutions. Its purpose seems to be the arousal of anger as it states, "In the beginning was the word/ And the word was Death/ And the word was nigger." The concluding lines once again address the list of the fallen heroes of the period.

Two of the best of Giovanni's entire repertoire are included in this selection and are without political overtones. They are the slightly sentimental remembrances of her childhood viewed in "Nikki-Rosa" and "Knoxville, Tennessee." In "Nikki-Rosa" the poet suspects that white reviewers and biographers will in the future likely discuss her childhood as one of hardship and poverty without understanding that love and family are compensation. Written eight days after the assassination of Dr. Martin Luther King, Jr., "Nikki-Rosa" says that "Black love is Black wealth." Although Giovanni essentially grew up in the North, she considers the South, as depicted in the poem "Knoxville, Tennessee," her spiritual home. The poem offers a look back at the times she spent with her grandparents, citing food and warmth as equated with love and spiritual nourishment.

**Analysis.** Although Giovanni's radical, reactive poetry gained the most critical attention and likely the widest readership, less than half of

Giovanni's work often echoed the radical spirit of her times. Here, members of the Black Panthers, a militant black empowerment group, demonstrate in Oakland, California, in 1968. They call for the release of their leader, Huey Newton, who was accused of killing a police officer.

the twenty-six poems in the collection could be viewed as revolutionary. Because the political poems drew the most notoriety, critics would later accuse Giovanni of "selling out" when her work began to take a less militant stance. Those reviewers apparently overlooked other selections in this volume that sentimentalized childhood, lauded music, or dealt with female identity.

Additionally, within the political selections, there are veiled hints that all was not as it should be, implying that much of the movement was spent in endless, undirected conversation without accomplishment. For example in "Poem (for TW)," the lines "You gave me a small coke/ And some large talk about being Black" lend an accusatory tone of inaction to the dialogue.

The group ethic of 1960s activism slowly gave way to the more individual concerns of the 1970s. Betye Saar's *Watching* captures the isolation many felt. In her poem "Cotton Candy on a Rainy Day," Giovanni wrote, "What this decade will be / known for / There is no doubt . . . it is / loneliness."

### SOURCES FOR FURTHER STUDY

Inge, Tonette Bond, ed. *Southern Women Writers: The New Generation.* Tuscaloosa: University of Alabama Press, 1990.

Robinson, Anna T. *Nikki Giovanni: From Revolution to Revelation.* Columbus: State Library of Ohio, 1979.

Weixlmann, Joe, and Chester J. Fontenot, eds. *Studies in Black American Literature.* Vol. 2 in *Belief Versus Theory in Black American Literary Criticism.* Greenwood, Fla.: Penkevill, 1986.

## COTTON CANDY ON A RAINY DAY

**Genre:** Poetry
**Subgenre:** Reflections
**Published:** New York, 1978
**Time period:** 1970s
**Setting:** United States

**Themes and Issues:** Written in the 1970s, this collection is Giovanni's darkest vision, reflecting, no doubt, the decade's cynicism and political disillusionment. A sense of futility permeates the work, perhaps due to the burgeoning of the political right combined with the personal catastrophe of her father's illness and ultimate death. The primary themes of the collection are aging, change, and unfulfilled dreams.

**The Poems.** The poems in this collection bespeak a tempering of Giovanni's previous vision. In a decade known for loneliness and disillusionment, the title poem likens life to cotton candy, "The sweet soft essence/ of possibility/ Never quite maturing." Giovanni seems to be coming to terms with unfulfilled potential, or, as she phrases it, "the unrealized dream of an idea unborn." In one selection, "Being and Nothingness (to quote a philosopher)," she laments that she was proud in being "a child of the 60s," but that decade is over "so that makes being nothing."

**Analysis.** The decade of the 1970s appeared to contradict many of the advances made in the 1960s toward civil rights and universal equality and produced in many of the earlier activists an overwhelming sense of loneliness. Gone was the camaraderie of the various social movements, leaving only a sense of futile aloneness. Concern over her father's health forced Giovanni to question her own mortality, and several of the selections refer not only to growing old but also to the ephemeral quality of life. The title of the work offers cotton candy as a metaphor for life. Cotton candy, like life, takes time to create and disappears quickly, melting away in the rain of years. Although the majority of the work is depressingly disenchanted, Giovanni's idealism is occasionally visible.

### SOURCES FOR FURTHER STUDY

Giddings, Paula. Introduction to *Cotton Candy on a Rainy Day*, by Nikki Giovanni. New York: William Morrow, 1978.

Rankine-Galloway, Honora. "Nikki Giovanni." In *Critical Survey of Poetry: English Language Series*, edited by Frank N. Magill. Rev. ed. Vol 3. Pasadena, Calif.: Salem Press, 1992.

Tate, Claudia, ed. *Black Women Writers at Work*. New York: Continuum, 1983.

### RE: CREATION
 **Genre:** Poetry
 **Subgenre:** Psychological introspection
 **Published:** Detroit, 1970
 **Time period:** Late 1960s
 **Setting:** United States

**Themes and Issues.** For some, *Re: Creation* is a marked departure from Giovanni's earlier work, because its focus is directed away from the larger struggle and more toward family and relationships. Composed during her pregnancy and published shortly after the birth of her son, the poems in this collection explore a woman's need to seek and to define her own identity. One reviewer in *Black World* magazine noted that Giovanni seemed "transformed into an almost declawed, tamed Panther with bad teeth"; however, Giovanni asserts her intention to find her own artistic direction. The central theme of the collection is the search for female identity, with motherhood being an important aspect of that identity. In one of the poems she notes that the birth of her son had defined her nature. She depicts motherhood as liberating, a view that, in itself, was considered radical.

**The Poems.** Two of the selections in this volume are juxtaposed companion pieces, "All I Gotta Do" and the often anthologized "Master Charge Blues." The first appears to illustrate the traditional role of women, which is "to sit and wait/ cause i'm a woman." In contrast, "Master Charge Blues" sets a lighter tone as the modern counterpoint exclaims, "ain't gonna let this get me down/ gonna take my master charge/ and get everything in town."

The best poem in the collection is "Ego-Tripping." Revealing the stereotypes of woman as mother, nurturer, and protector, the poem challenges women to throw off the old images and re-create themselves. In many lines, the poem makes connections to Africa and offers images of the continent as woman, mother, and fodder for tourists.

**Analysis.** Although most of the poems in this collection are introspective, many are dedicated to other women, primarily singers such as Lena Horne, Diana Ross, Dionne Warwick, Nina Simone, and Aretha Franklin. Giovanni declares her need to seek her own vision as an artist and poetically encourages other women to nurture themselves as well.

### SOURCES FOR FURTHER STUDY

Blain, Virginia, et al. *The Feminist Companion to Literature in English*. New Haven, Conn.: Yale University Press, 1990.

Robert Gwathmey's 1945 oil painting *Lullaby* reflects the strength of motherhood, a state Giovanni found liberating. The center of her universe, Giovanni's son gave her writing a new direction. Her redefined role as a poet is evident in *Re: Creation*, her 1970 collection of poems.

Jago, Carol. *Nikki Giovanni in the Classroom: "The Same Ol' Danger but a Brand New Pleasure."* Urbana, Ill.: National Council of Teachers of English, 1999.

Noble, Jean. *Beautiful, Also, Are the Souls of My Black Sisters: A History of the Black Woman in America.* Englewood Cliffs, N.J.: Prentice-Hall, 1978.

## THOSE WHO RIDE THE NIGHT WINDS

**Genre:** Poetry
**Subgenre:** Social commentary
**Published:** New York, 1983
**Time period:** 1970s and 1980s
**Setting:** United States

**Themes and Issues.** This collection, Giovanni's first for adults since *Cotton Candy on a Rainy Day*, reflects a renewed sense of hope and wisdom. The poems are more reflective than those in the previous volume and seem more concerned with the courage and dedication of those who have attempted to reach their goals, regardless of outcomes. The poems focus on public figures instead of personal issues.

**The Poems.** The work is divided into two sections: night winds and day trippers. The former is serious; the latter, lighter in tone. The night has a negative connotation, conjuring images of night riders, men in white robes who ride lathered horses through the community. In contrast, the light of day reveals all.

Selections in the night winds section are dedicated to a variety of well-known persons. "This Is Not for John Lennon" refers to John Lennon of the British rock group the Beatles, who was murdered outside his apartment building for no apparent reason other than his fame. The title of the poem refers to the fact that Lennon is merely the victim of a society that feels compelled to obliterate its heroes. In another selection, Giovanni

creates the analogy of a tree to discuss the assassination of Robert Kennedy. She asserts that people would not cut down a tree before it had outlived its usefulness but those same people think nothing of the unnatural act of killing someone in his prime.

"Mirrors (for Billie Jean King)" discusses a different kind of assassination. King, a professional tennis champion, was attacked by the press and the public for her sexual orientation. In the poem, Giovanni praises King's composure in handling the issue and laments society's tendency to make private lives public. Another poem depicts the ways in which society downplays the feats of certain individuals. "Harvest (for Rosa Parks)" discusses the heroism of the

Giovanni refuses to allow her readers to forget the past, presenting images of the night riders, members of the Ku Klux Klan who formed lynching parties that seized and murdered innocent blacks. Horace Pippin's 1943 oil painting *Mr. Prejudice* (Philadelphia Museum of Art: Gift of Dr. and Mrs. Matthew T. Moore) recalls these atrocities. A hooded figure dressed in white lurks in the upper right.

woman who refused to give up her seat on a Montgomery, Alabama, bus and is credited with launching the Civil Rights movement. Giovanni states that Parks knew where "to plant" her feet on that day.

**Analysis.** In the collection Giovanni alters her tone as well as her style. She explores new territory by employing a lineless form, using groups of words separated by ellipses. The poems appear as paragraphs of continuous lines with ellipses indicating something omitted or missing in the context. For the first time, Giovanni capitalizes the personal pronoun "I," perhaps as an indication of a newly acquired acceptance of self coupled with a maturity of artistic vision.

## SOURCES FOR FURTHER STUDY

Fowler, Virginia C. *Nikki Giovanni.* New York: Twayne Publishers, 1992.

Mitchell, Mozella G. "Nikki Giovanni." In *Dictionary of Literary Biography.* Vol. 41 in *African American Poets Since 1955,* edited by Trudier Harris and Thadious M. Davis. Detroit: Gale Research, 1985.

Rankine-Galloway, Honora. "Nikki Giovanni." In *Critical Survey of Poetry: English Language Series,* edited by Frank N. Magill. Rev. ed. Vol 3. Pasadena, Calif.: Salem Press, 1992.

*Other Works*

**A DIALOGUE: JAMES BALDWIN AND NIKKI GIOVANNI** (1973). One of two "conversation" books in Nikki Giovanni's canon, this volume is the record of a running discussion between her and James Baldwin, the African American novelist of works such as *Go Tell It on the Mountain* (1953) and *The Fire Next Time* (1963). This dialogue brings together two generations of black artists, male and female. Much of the conversation revolves around personal reminiscences, the seemingly separate role development of black men and women, and the responsibility of the artist to depict life truthfully.

**GEMINI: AN EXTENDED AUTOBIOGRAPHICAL STATEMENT ON MY FIRST TWENTY-FIVE YEARS OF BEING A BLACK POET** (1971). This autobiographical collection of essays was published when Giovanni was thirty-three years old, a seemingly early age for an autobiography. However, Giovanni had already experienced, through her involvement in the Civil Rights movement and the birth of her son, many significant moments in her country's and her own personal history.

*Gemini* is Giovanni's most widely reviewed book, and in it, as in her entire body of work, she intermingles personal and public history. She also uses this forum as a means of addressing one of the persistent themes in her poetry, that of the role of a woman, particularly a black woman, in the world.

**A POETIC EQUATION: CONVERSATIONS BETWEEN NIKKI GIOVANNI AND MARGARET WALKER** (1974). In 1972 Nikki Giovanni and Margaret Walker, the poet, novelist, and author of *Jubilee* (1966), were invited to read from their works at the Paul Laurence Dunbar Centennial at the University of Dayton in Ohio. This book, which transcribes the subsequent conversation between the authors, is the result of that joint appearance. Although this work lacks the gender diversity of the conversation with Baldwin, it is nonetheless interesting in presenting the definite views of racial strife of two women separated only by age.

**RACISM 101** (1994). Giovanni wrote this collection of essays after accepting a permanent position at the largely conservative Virginia

"I'm a big fan of the black woman," Giovanni once said, "and so I'm always looking at aspects of the black woman—what she's doing and how she does it." Barkley Hendricks's 1970 portrait *Lawdy Mama* (The Studio Museum in Harlem, New York) offers a glimpse of one of these women Giovanni celebrates.

Polytechnic Institute. Her spirit of activism rings true, and the collection has been called a survival guide for African American students on predominantly white college campuses. Some of the essays contain good advice for students of all groups and professors as well. Never one to gloss over reality, Giovanni is critical of higher education for its failures and its tendency to perpetuate mythology instead of taking an active position to correct it. With inevitable historical touches and references to past leaders, *Racism 101* is essential reading for anyone who thinks the battles are over and the wars are won.

Betye Saar's 1999 piece *Equality* spoofs some of the stereotypes about black speech that persist to this day. For Giovanni, however, dialect and black lingo lend her work the spark of realism and immediacy.

**SHIMMY SHIMMY SHIMMY LIKE MY SISTER KATE: LOOKING AT THE HARLEM RENAISSANCE THROUGH POEMS** (1996). During the 1920s, African American artists, writers, and musicians migrated from the South to the North seeking greater freedom of expression. Many gathered in a section of Manhattan called Harlem. The flowering of artistic expression from that region became known as the Harlem Renaissance, which popularized some of the best-known African American writers, such as Langston Hughes, Richard Wright, and Gwendolyn Brooks. This book, designed primarily for young readers, is a poetic tribute to those artists and to the extraordinary work they produced.

## Resources

Sources of interest to students of Nikki Giovanni include the following:

**Poetry Recordings.** Giovanni has recorded many of her poetry collections, in which she combines spoken word readings of her work with gospel and blues music. The following are available: *In Philadelphia* (1997); *Way I Feel* (1995), including "My House," "The Way I Feel," "When I Die," "Revolutionary Dreams," and "The Life I Led"; *Like a Ripple on a Pond* (1993), including "Legacies," "Pass Me Not," "Deep River," "Africa II," "Like A Ripple on a Pond," and "I'm Glad"; and *Truth Is on Its Way* (1993), including "Nikki-Rosa," "Alabama Poem," "Ego-Tripping," "Woman Poem," and "Poem for a Lady of Leisure Now Retired."

**Nikki Giovanni Home Page.** Giovanni's own World Wide Web home page at Virginia Polytechnic Institute contains up-to-date biographical information, awards listings, publication information, and details about cultural events sponsored by her classes at VPI. (http://athena.english.vt.edu/Giovanni/Nikki_Giovanni.html)

**The Academy of American Poets, Poetry Exhibits, Nikki Giovanni.** The Academy of American Poets has an informative Web site with a selected bibliography of Giovanni's work, poems, and links to other Giovanni sites. (http://www.poets.org/poets/poets.cfm?prmlD=176)

*JOYCE DUNCAN*

# Lorraine Hansberry

**BORN:** May 19, 1930, Chicago, Illinois
**DIED:** January 12, 1965, New York, New York
**IDENTIFICATION:** Mid-twentieth-century playwright known for her depiction of the plight of the inner-city black American struggling to escape the ghetto and attain the so-called American Dream.

Lorraine Hansberry was the youngest and first African American writer to win the New York Drama Critics Circle Award for her critically acclaimed and popularly received drama *A Raisin in the Sun* (1959). This play is a curriculum staple in high schools for its raw and complex portrayal of a struggling African American family confronting issues that impact the nature of black identity in an America still fraught with racism and prejudice. Hansberry's most famous work, this drama stands as an icon for the Civil Rights movement of the 1950s and 1960s and has had numerous productions and two film treatments.

Lorraine Vivian Hansberry was born on May 19, 1930, on the South Side of Chicago, Illinois, the last of four children born to Carl Augustus and Nanny (Perry) Hansberry. As she describes in her autobiography, *To Be Young, Gifted, and Black: Lorraine Hansberry in Her Own Words* (1969), her parents were "utilitarian" in their attitude toward their children, who were raised with strong attitudes that promoted good morals and ensured success. Hansberry stated that, until her father's death, the children's needs were superbly met. She and her brothers had more possessions and more "cash" than their peers—"but that was all. . . . Of love and my parents, there is little to be written."

**Childhood.** Hansberry recounts a relatively happy, though complex, childhood. Separated from her other siblings by seven years, she quickly "learned to play alone." Second, because her father was a successful real-estate businessman, she found herself labeled as the "rich girl" in her South Side Chicago neighborhood. Better dressed and more affluent than the other children at her school, she was taunted by them and became, ironically, jealous of their streetwise knowledge. She recounts fantasizing that her roller skate key was really a house key so that she could imitate the latchkey lifestyle of her schoolmates with working parents.

Hansberry's mother, Nanny, a former schoolteacher, often welcomed to the Hansberry

Women gather in the park in Allan Rohan Crite's 1941 oil painting *Shadow and Sunlight*. The Hansberrys were strong advocates of social change. Eventually they left their neighborhood, challenging Chicago's segregation laws by moving to an all-white section of town.

Showing their support for demonstrations against lunch-counter segregation in the South, members of the New York Youth Committee for Integration sit at a New York Woolworth's store counter on April 2, 1960, quietly reading newspapers as a form of protest. Hansberry, following in the footsteps of her parents, also became involved in movements to end discrimination.

home notable figures of the African American community. Both of Hansberry's parents were continually involved in political matters; her father ran for Congress and her mother was a ward committeewoman. They were also intensely associated with causes supporting African American rights. From early on, Hansberry was immersed in an intellectual environment dedicated to social and political change.

**The Future Writer.** Hansberry's father, Carl, was a realtor and a deeply committed civil rights proponent who was very active in the National Association for the Advancement of Colored People (NAACP). He spent a great deal of his time and money fighting unfair and discriminatory housing practices. In her autobiography, Hansberry indicates that Carl became embittered and was driven to an early death when, after dedicating much of his life toward improving ghetto conditions and even winning a Supreme Court decision, he saw

that his efforts had done little to better the housing problems of Chicago's African American residents.

Hansberry further describes an incident when she was eight years old and living with her family in a hostile white neighborhood, in which she nearly lost her life to a mob that surrounded her house and tossed bricks and concrete pieces inside, one of which barely missed her head. These early experiences formed a background for her plays—all of which deal with the human struggle for freedom, completion, and a happiness based on real values.

**College Years.** After graduating from Englewood High School in 1948, Hansberry decided to attend the University of Wisconsin to study art. She disliked many of the required subjects that she felt were irrelevant to her goals, but she flourished in her literature, philosophy, and art classes. After viewing a Sean O'Casey play, Hansberry's focus was changed forever. She reportedly felt "a melody" within and an impetus to "write one in a different key." It was this feeling that prompted her ultimately to leave the university in 1950 and to move to New York City "to pursue an education of another kind."

**The Fledgling Writer.** After moving to the Lower East Side of New York, Hansberry explored the life of Greenwich Village and the ghettos of Harlem. She educated herself politically by participating in peace and freedom movements, picket lines, street-corner speeches, and delegations for the needy or unjustly accused. She also began to work as a receptionist, typist, and writer for the actor-activist Paul Robeson's "new Negro paper" *Freedom*, which she termed "*the* journal of Negro liberation." By 1952 she had become an associate editor, expanding her skills as a reviewer of African American books and plays. In the same year, at only twenty-two, she replaced Robeson as representative to the Interconti-nental Peace Congress in Montevideo, Uruguay. There she gained a global perspective on issues of race and gender discrimination.

**Marriage and Domestic Life.** In 1953 Hansberry married Robert Nemiroff, a white writer, producer, and social activist whom she had met at a protest rally at New York University. In the same year she resigned her position at *Freedom* and committed herself to full-time dramatic writing. During the subsequent three years, she had three plays in progress while holding part-time office, theater, and garment-industry jobs. After her husband completed his education, Hansberry was able to dedicate herself to full-time writing. Although the marriage is reported to have been happy, the couple divorced in 1964, but their association continued professionally. Hansberry made Nemiroff her literary executor, trusting his judgment in adapting and producing her work.

**The Turning Point.** In 1957 Hansberry read a scene of her newly completed play to some of her husband's theatrical colleagues, who immediately wanted to produce it. However, support for a Broadway play with a black playwright, black director, and predominantly black cast was not forthcoming. However, *A Raisin in the Sun*, starring Sidney Poitier and Ruby Dee, finally opened on Broadway in March 1959 to excellent critical reviews. Almost overnight Hansberry became a theatrical celebrity.

**Last Years.** A film version of *A Raisin in the Sun*, for which Hansberry wrote the screenplay, was released by Columbia Pictures in 1961. She subsequently wrote *The Drinking Gourd* (1972) for a televised series on the Civil War. The program was never televised, but her teleplay was published posthumously in 1972.

Greenwich Village in 1966. The New York City neighborhood, an old stomping ground of Hansberry's, was swiftly becoming an enclave for artists, writers, and political activists.

# HIGHLIGHTS IN HANSBERRY'S LIFE

**1930**   Lorraine Vivian Hansberry is born on May 19 in Chicago, Illinois.

**1948**   Graduates from Englewood High School; enters the University of Wisconsin.

**1950**   Moves to New York City; writes for *Freedom* magazine.

**1953**   Marries Robert Nemiroff.

**1953–1956**   Holds a series of part-time jobs while writing; has three plays in progress.

**1957**   Completes *A Raisin in the Sun*, which is originally rejected for production.

**1959**   *A Raisin in the Sun* opens on Broadway.

**1961**   *A Raisin in the Sun* wins special award at Cannes Film Festival.

**1963**   Hansberry is hospitalized for tests and diagnosed with cancer; meets with Attorney General Robert Kennedy to discuss racial crisis in America.

**1964**   Divorces husband, who remains professionally involved in artistic projects; *The Sign in Sidney Brustein's Window* opens in New York.

**1965**   Hansberry dies of cancer at age thirty-four on January 12 in New York City.

**1969**   Her autobiography, *To Be Young, Gifted, and Black*, is published in book form and adapted for the theater.

**1970**   *Les Blancs* opens in New York.

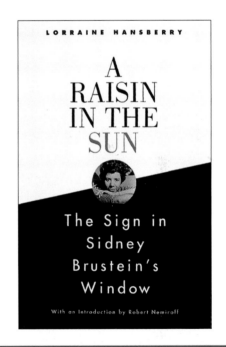

In 1963 Hansberry was hospitalized for tests and eventually diagnosed with cancer. She valiantly continued her political work, meeting with Attorney General Robert Kennedy to discuss the racial crisis in America. She also continued her work on several plays and wrote the text for a pictorial work on the Civil Rights movement. Her play *The Sign in Sidney Brustein's Window* opened in October 1964, to mixed and contradictory reviews. Friends and admirers respectfully raised money to keep the play running for 101 performances, to the very day of its author's death. On January 12, 1965, Hansberry, a mere thirty-four years of age, succumbed to her illness.

Lorraine Hansberry was primarily a dramatist. Her view of the world was filtered through the depiction of ideas and emotions on a three-dimensional stage. Even her well-known and intellectually stimulating autobiography is punctuated by a variety of scenes from her own plays. In her few artistically productive years, Hansberry produced a classic play, several controversial dramas, a highly imaginative autobiography, and a pictorial docudrama on the high price of the civil rights struggle. Overall, however, she is most remembered for her play *A Raisin in the Sun*, depicting the powerful ideas and emotions of an African American family in crisis, who reveal themselves to be supremely human and are universally understood by audiences wherever the play is produced.

**Issues in Hansberry's Plays.** Central issues in Hansberry's plays revolve around what it means to be a fully actualized human being in a complex and limiting world. That world may be one of oppressive racial prejudice or one of self-created apathy, where characters fight their own desperation in order to become their own best selves. Yet this "highest self" is always set in a social context—a defining time and place. Hansberry, in her writings, implies that art must always be a social statement.

Walter Younger, the protagonist of *A Raisin in the Sun*, lives in an African American ghetto. His plight is rooted both in this fact and in the fact that he believes in American materialism as the means by which he will actualize himself. Sidney Brustein, of *The Sign in Sidney Brustein's*

In Jacob Getlar Smith's oil painting *Snow Shovellers,* a group of laborers heads out to try and earn some extra money. Ghetto life was often marked by the recurring cycle of poverty and the lack of well-paying jobs. It was hard for black families to stake a claim on the middle class, which was assumed to be a status reserved only for whites.

*Window*, faces disillusionment and paralyzing apathy but, through uncompromising self-analysis, finds an authentic existence that is both life affirming and socially conscious.

**People in Hansberry's Plays.** Although Hansberry is categorized as an African American writer, she is also contradictorily termed a "universal" writer. Early reviews of *A Raisin in the Sun* applauded the work because it was not only "a Negro play, it was a play about people." Hansberry responded with her usual penetrating wit that "I'd always been under the impression that Negroes *are* people."

The core of the problem—the assumption that plays by black writers must be limited to the discussion of race issues—identifies clearly how Hansberry creates the people in her plays. Her characters are recognizable in their universal human traits and needs, yet they live in a specific time, place, and historical moment. Hansberry herself proclaimed that, in order to create a universal character, one must clearly create the specific character: "Universality emerges from truthful identity of what is." Thus, the people in her plays are very specific human beings who transcend stereotypical categories and become universally relatable.

Hansberry's characters also run the gamut of the social classes. *A Raisin in the Sun* is peopled by members of a lower-middle-class family and a Nigerian intellectual. The voices of the educated and financially secure characters often comment on the struggles of the working class: The African Asagai in *A Raisin in the Sun* implies that Walter Younger's struggle is the expression of a worldwide movement for human liberation.

**Heroism through Action.** Quite clearly, Walter Younger in *A Raisin in the Sun* believes that he is not allowed his inherited right—the right to be a successful black man in a white man's world, a world peopled by "takers."

Walter's defining moment is when he decides to move into his mother's new house in a racist white neighborhood, refusing financial gain he would make by staying away. It is the moment when he becomes a hero—to his mother, family, himself, and to the audience. Another example of heroic action and decision is when Sidney Brustein wrestles with his own apathy and indifference, engendered by his Jewishness and personal experiences. His heroic decision is simply to continue to strive and to take a stand against evil in the world.

**Hansberry and Film.** In 1960 Hansberry was contracted to write the screenplay for *A Raisin in the Sun* to be produced by Columbia Pictures. She subsequently produced two versions that were substantially different from the play, each including scenes that provided a harsher indict-

Hansberry's fresh and provocative voice arrived on Broadway in 1959 with the debut of *A Raisin in the Sun*. Flanked by Ruby Dee (left) and Diana Sands (right), Sydney Poitier played the role of Walter Younger, a frustrated chauffeur who points to an elusive freedom that is just out of reach.

ment of the American social system that marginalized and oppressed black citizens. Neither version was accepted by the studio, which chose a third, shortened version. Despite this fact, her work received a special award at the Cannes Film Festival in France in 1961.

The film, starring Sidney Poitier and Ruby Dee, who reprised their Broadway roles, remains a powerful rendition of the play. A second film production starring Danny Glover was presented on television by American Playhouse in 1989 and includes the complete text.

**Hansberry's Literary Legacy.** Hansberry's untimely death prevented much of her other work besides *A Raisin in the Sun* from being readily produced, filmed, and published. Her insight and foresight predicted many of the controversial aspects of the pan-African movement and the post-1960s African American identity crisis.

Hansberry was a pioneer who depicted basic and often shocking truths about the plight of African Americans in a country that continued to fail them. She was an artist who portrayed both the loneliness and the grandeur of the African American struggle to forge a sense of identity and empowerment. Her concept of failure of the American Dream is one of misplaced values, not one of a moral decline and careless irresponsibility. She professes that African Americans must challenge the system with heroic individualism and stand up for what is right, authentic, and forward moving before subscribing to the materialism of a capitalist society.

## BIBLIOGRAPHY

Abramson, Doris E. *Negro Playwrights in the American Theatre, 1925–1959*. New York: Columbia University Press, 1969.

Bigsby, C. W. E. *Confrontation and Commitment: A Study of Contemporary Drama, 1959–1966*. Columbia: University of Missouri Press, 1968.

Cheney, Anne. *Lorraine Hansberry*. Boston: Twayne Publishers, 1984.

Cruse, Harold. *The Crisis of the Negro Intellectual*. New York: William Morrow, 1967.

Hansberry, Lorraine. *To Be Young, Gifted, and Black: Lorraine Hansberry in Her Own Words*. Adapted by Robert Nemiroff. Englewood Cliffs, N.J.: Prentice-Hall, 1969.

Kaiser, Ernest, and Robert Nemiroff. "A Lorraine Hansberry Bibliography." *Freedomways* 19 (Fourth Quarter, 1979). This issue is devoted to the work of Lorraine Hansberry.

McKissack, Patricia C., and Fredrick L. McKissack. *Young, Black, and Determined: A Biography of Lorraine Hansberry*. New York: Holiday House, 1997.

Noble, Jeanne L. *Beautiful, Also, Are the Souls of My Black Sisters: A History of the Black Women in America*. New York: Prentice-Hall, 1978.

Scheader, Catherine. *Lorraine Hansberry: Playwright and Voice of Justice*. New York: Enslow Publishers, 1998.

## SOME INSPIRATIONS BEHIND HANSBERRY'S WORK

Lorraine Hansberry's uncle William Leo Hansberry was a scholar of African antiquity, whose students included Nigerian princes; his ideas undoubtedly influenced her artistic concerns. She also studied under W. E. B. Du Bois, the famous author who is considered the father of pan-Africanism, the idea or advocacy of a union of all the African nations.

Hansberry worked closely with the singer and actor Paul Robeson, who was associated with communism, and she was consistently involved in the black freedom struggle. Hansberry's ideas were molded by the intellectual heritage of her parents and their struggles in the Civil Rights movement, her education, and the dynamic experiences she underwent during her college and working years.

## A RAISIN IN THE SUN

**Genre:** Play
**Subgenre:** Social drama
**Produced:** New York, 1959
**Time period:** 1950s
**Setting:** South Side of Chicago, Illinois

**Themes and Issues.** Racism and prejudice in the suburban United States are the obvious issues in Lorraine Hansberry's masterpiece and prizewinning drama *A Raisin in the Sun*. Initially entitled "The Crystal Stair," after a poem by Langston Hughes, the play's title was changed to a part of a line from Hughes's poem "Harlem," from his volume *Montage of a Dream Deferred*. The powerful short poem encapsulates the terrible truth about oppression—that it crushes people's aspirations and causes them to become desperate: "What happens to a dream deferred?/ Does it dry up/ Like a raisin in the sun?"

The issue of racism is never overtly mentioned until late in the play, when Mr. Lindner, a representative of the white suburban neighborhood to which the Youngers are planning to move, approaches the family and offers substantial financial gain if they will abort their plans to move. Instead, the matter of race and how it can limit one's possibilities is subtly interwoven in the dramatic exchanges among the main characters and how they react to one another on a personal level. The members of the Younger family are defined by their experiences as African American people as well as by their hopes, dreams, and aspirations. They are a family in financial crisis who must decide whether to fight or be overpowered by circumstances.

**The Plot.** The central conflict for the Younger family—matriarch Lena, oldest son Walter Lee, sister Beneatha, Walter's wife Ruth, and their son Travis—is the arrival of a ten-thousand-dollar check that Lena receives from her deceased husband's insurance policy. Although it is his mother's money, Walter, who has long deferred his dream of becoming independent and leaving his chauffeuring job, immediately assumes that he should have the money to buy into a liquor store business with two friends. Lena, however, has plans of her own for the money. She hopes to finance Beneatha's medical education and to buy a home far from the crowded ghetto apartment that the family has rented for many years.

Patrons huddle over their books in Jacob Lawrence's 1960 painting *The Library*. Through education Beneatha attempts to reject the limits placed on her race and her gender in Hansberry's drama *A Raisin in the Sun*.

Through a series of conversations and confrontations, the audience learns that Ruth is pregnant with a second child and, because of financial pressures, is contemplating abortion. Beneatha is attending college and is dating both a prosperous middle-class merchant's son, George Murchison, and a Nigerian intellectual, Joseph Asagai, who inspires her connection with her African roots. The two women—one who dedicates herself to her family by working at menial jobs, and the other, who is the family's great hope for the future—reveal two sides of the American work ethic. The audience also sees the many sides of Walter. He despairs over the dashing of his dreams to succeed. He is exhilarated when Lena entrusts him with the funds left over after her down payment on a house—more than six thousand dollars, some of which he is instructed to put away for Beneatha's education.

Betraying Lena's good will, Walter entrusts all of the money to his investor friends, Willy and Bobo. In a scene that demonstrates the depths of Walter's desperation, Bobo reveals that Willy has absconded with the money. Lena tearfully berates her son, beating him in the face and assailing him with the words: "I see him grow thin and old before he was forty. . . . killing himself. . . . and you give it all away in a day."

In the final scenes, Lena, recovering her senses, remonstrates with Walter not to cave in and accept Linder's offer. She communicates that money is not what the Younger family is about, that there is something more important inside them. Walter, however, disagrees and calls Lindner back, apparently to renegotiate. When Lindner arrives, Walter switches his position and gives a poignant speech about why the Youngers will move into a neighborhood that seeks to exclude them.

**Analysis.** *A Raisin in the Sun* is often misunderstood as a chronicle of an African American family aspiring to middle-class values. However, the drama is really about discovering dignity through conflict and making the choice to strive for what is best in oneself. Walter Younger undergoes a metamorphosis from basing his sense of power and reality on material

## PLAYS

1959 A Raisin in the Sun
1964 The Sign in Sidney Brustein's Window
1969 To Be Young, Gifted, and Black
1970 Les Blancs, ed. Robert Nemiroff
1972 The Drinking Gourd, ed. Robert Nemiroff
1972 What Use Are Flowers?: A Fable in One Act, ed. Robert Nemiroff
1972 Les Blancs: The Collected Last Plays of Lorraine Hansberry (includes Les Blancs, The Drinking Gourd, and What Use Are Flowers?)

## SCREENPLAYS

1960 A Raisin in the Sun

## NONFICTION

1964 The Movement: Documentary of a Struggle for Equality
1969 To Be Young, Gifted, and Black: Lorraine Hansberry in Her Own Words, ed. Robert Nemiroff

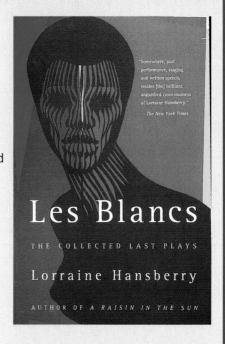

"Somewhere, past performance, staging and written speech, resides [the] brilliant, anguished consciousness of Lorraine Hansberry."
—*The New York Times*

Les Blancs

THE COLLECTED LAST PLAYS

Lorraine Hansberry

AUTHOR OF *A RAISIN IN THE SUN*

values to understanding that he, a black man, can be a social force.

Walter decides that he will move into the white neighborhood because it is the right thing to do. He will still have to make enough money to keep the new house, and he and his family will probably face verbal and physical violence, but this no longer seems to be the issue for him. He has found his spiritual core, a core that was missing as long as he envisioned himself in terms of money. Lena confides to Ruth as they finish packing the moving crates: "He finally come into his manhood today, didn't he?"

The insurance check is a central symbol in the play, and the loss of the money is necessary for Walter to come to terms with himself. Although Walter betrays his mother's trust, he does it out of hope for a dream too long deferred. To be an American is to subscribe to the American Dream and to be tempted by its materialism. Walter should have the right to attain that dream, but not, Hansberry warns, at the expense of self. Thus, Hansberry takes a universal insight that acts as a cautionary tale for all Americans and wraps it in the particular dramatization of one African American family. The Youngers not only find a way to continue the social struggle for African American equality but also, in the process, come to a new sense of self-awareness.

## SOURCES FOR FURTHER STUDY

Baraka, Amiri. Introduction. In *A Raisin in the Sun*, by Lorraine Hansberry. Reprint. New York: New American Library, 1987.

Miller, Jeanne-Marie. "Measure Him Right." In *Teaching American Ethnic Literatures: Nineteen Essays*. Albuquerque: University of New Mexico Press, 1996.

Parks, Sheri. "In My Mother's House: Black Feminist Aesthetics, Television, and *A Raisin in the Sun*." In *Theatre and Feminist Aesthetics*, edited by Karen Laughlin and Catherine Schuler. Madison, N.J.: Fairleigh Dickinson University Press, 1995.

## THE SIGN IN SIDNEY BRUSTEIN'S WINDOW

**Genre:** Play
**Subgenre:** Social drama
**Produced:** New York, 1964
**Time period:** Early 1960s
**Setting:** Greenwich Village, New York City

**Themes and Issues.** The theme of alienation from self and society is a particularly modern one, which Hansberry utilizes in *The Sign in Sidney Brustein's Window*. The play's characters, unlike those in *A Raisin in the Sun*, are primarily white. They are liberal artists and intellectuals who struggle not against an oppressive external social system but against a depressive internal isolation that prevents them from connecting to themselves and others. Because

Kathryn Jacobi's oil painting *Gospel Singer, Study #3* evokes the quiet strength of Lena, whose dream of improving the lives of her family was not derailed by the racism and antagonism that surrounded her. "I was born black and female," Hansberry once said. These twin identities influenced and helped to shape her work.

these characters have lost touch with themselves and one another, they are unable to take any kind of stand in the outside world.

The protagonist Sidney, once active in political causes, is apparently numbed by disillusionment and personal failures and is no longer involved in his previous activities. He wears a mask of cynicism and emotionally abuses his wife, Iris, an aspiring actress, who is the nearest object of contempt for his own bitterness and self-hate. With this play, Hansberry hoped to reengage American intellectuals in the struggle for human rights; it is a warning for them to stop retreating from the world before the world is lost.

**The Plot.** Sidney Brustein buys a small newspaper that he hopes to run. The course of the play reveals Sidney's troubled marriage and his general loss of faith in the human race and in humanity's power to evolve. Although there is little action and much dialogue, the audience gradually learns that Sidney hopes to redeem himself by backing a political candidate through whom he hopes the corrupt local political machine can be defeated. Once Sidney sees the candidate unmasked as a willing pawn of the corrupt system and watches his sister-in-law die of an apparently intentional drug overdose, he decides to take a stand and oppose the system through newspaper editorials.

**Analysis.** *The Sign in Sidney Brustein's Window* was not well received and was quite a surprise to fans of Hansberry who expected a "black play." However, Hansberry was identifying and universalizing a loss of faith in the human race and its power to direct its own destiny. With this play she

Hansberry's father saw his political ideals crushed, when he failed to improve significantly the living conditions of blacks in Chicago. He is a possible inspiration for the soured and cynical Sidney Brustein. In her play, Hansberry advocated action, as in this 1965 march in Montgomery, Alabama, led by Dr. Martin Luther King, Jr.

intended to inspire hope in its audiences. The play closed after 101 performances—kept alive by the support of Hansberry's friends and fellow artists. The last performance was held on the day she died.

## SOURCES FOR FURTHER STUDY

Carter, Steven. *Hansberry's Drama*. New York: Penguin, 1993.

Nemiroff, Robert. "The One Hundred and One Final Performances of *Sidney Brustein*." Introduction to *The Sign in Sidney Brustein's Window*, by Lorraine Hansberry. New York: Random House, 1965.

Wilkerson, Margaret, ed. *Nine Plays by Black Women*. New York: New American Library, 1986.

# Other Works

**LES BLANCS** (1970). The title of Lorraine Hansberry's controversial play *Les Blancs* (The Whites), was a response to a 1958 play by Jean Genet, *Les Nègres* (The Blacks). Hansberry's play demonstrates her abiding interest in Africa and what the revolutions there have to tell people about the racial and spiritual evolution of the human race. Hansberry was an avid student of African studies and saw an awareness of roots as a means by which African Americans could counteract their sense of isolation from a global community. The play concerns three brothers—Eric, Tshembe Matoseh, and Abioseh Matoseh—who clash over ideological and cultural concerns. The play itself was an attempt to address the problems of both racial and political divisions and to explore how the societies of the capitalist West and developing nations can unite and move forward.

**THE DRINKING GOURD** (1972). This play is a consciousness-raising depiction of the toll and tragedy of the economic and political system of American slavery and the measures taken to maintain it. Commissioned as a television production, it was to be part of a special report on the Civil War. The production was shelved, and Hansberry reclaimed the rights to the play for dramatic production. Excerpts are included in her autobiography and reflect the wonderful lyricism of the dialogue. The title itself refers to the system of secret signs, songs, and passwords that slaves employed to assist one another in escaping to freedom in the North. "Follow the Drinking Gourd" was a spiritual, a song of the Underground Railroad. In the context of the play it represents the path to freedom that never materializes for the protagonist.

Whitfield Lovell's 1999 installation *Whispers from the Walls* reflects many of the concerns Hansberry addresses in her writing—the importance of family and home, the struggles of the past informing the challenges of the present.

**THE MOVEMENT: DOCUMENTARY OF A STRUGGLE FOR EQUALITY** (1964). A photographic record of the price of hate, this volume combines pictures from a variety of photographers with Hansberry's commentary. The sometimes shocking photos document the phases of the Civil Rights movement, arranged in a meaningful sequence. Supporting Hansberry's text are carefully chosen quotes from black leaders such as the early-nineteenth-century revolutionary Nat Turner and the escaped slave and abolitionist Frederick Douglass.

**TO BE YOUNG, GIFTED, AND BLACK: LORRAINE HANSBERRY IN HER OWN WORDS** (1969). Hansberry's creative autobiography is an amalgam of personal reflections, anecdotes, comments, and scenes from her plays. The volume has an internal logic of its own that provides glimpses into her inner world. A sense of the "true" Lorraine Hansberry is revealed through her insightful and profound observations.

The foreword includes an oft-quoted passage from Hansberry's 1959 speech to her fellow writers, "The Negro Writer and His Roots," which indicates the central motivating impulse for her art. She recognizes an innate goodness and responsive possibility in the world: "I wish to live because life has within it that which is good, that which is beautiful, and that which is love. . . . Moreover, because this is so, I wish others to live for generations and generations and generations and generations." Lorraine Hansberry lived a very short and intense life, and her spirit lives on in the continuing legacy of her dramatic renderings, which ask audiences to see, to evaluate, to feel, and finally, to hope.

**WHAT USE ARE FLOWERS?** (1972). This short drama of five scenes, subtitled *A Fable in One Act*, presents a surrealistic scenario of a world that has been mostly destroyed by atomic blasts. The scenes consist of interactions between an old hermit who returns from the forest and a group of children that he educates about the meaning of civilization and the importance of preserving and respecting the process that created it.

## Resources

Lorraine Hansberry's papers are held by her ex-husband, Robert Nemiroff. Information about her may be found on line and on audio and video.

**Audio and Video.** *Lorraine Hansberry Speaks Out: Art and Black Revolution* (1972), edited by Nemiroff, is available from Caedmon Records. *To Be Young, Gifted, and Black*, adapted from the play based on Hansberry's autobiography, was produced by NET in January 1972. *A Raisin in the Sun* was filmed in 1961, starring Sydney Poitier, and in 1989, starring Danny Glover.

**The San Antonio College LitWeb Lorraine Hansberry Page.** This site provides much information about the author, with photos, a listing of works, and informative links to teaching *A Raisin in the Sun*, which may also be useful study guides for students. (http://www.accd.edu/sac/english/bailey/hansberr.htm)

**ISU Play Concordances.** This database provides the complete dialogue of *A Raisin in the Sun* indexed and annotated for textual context. It is valuable for itemized research and cross-referencing to other African American literary works. (http://www.public.iastate.edu/~spires/Concord/raisin.html)

**EducETH.** This is a Web site for students and teachers, with reading and teaching guides. It is also available for requests for information about Hansberry. (http://educeth.ethz.ch/english/readinglist/hansberryl)

*SHERRY MORTON-MOLLO*

# Ernest Hemingway

**BORN:** July 21, 1899, Oak Park, Illinois
**DIED:** July 2, 1961, Ketchum, Idaho
**IDENTIFICATION:** Probably the most widely read American writer of serious fiction in the twentieth century, famous for his simple writing style and repeated use of the theme of grace under pressure.

Ernest Hemingway wrote his most popular stories of expatriate Americans in Europe touched by the passion and pain of love and war during the 1930s and 1940s. Later in life, he won both a Pulitzer Prize and a Nobel Prize in literature for his powerful novella *The Old Man and the Sea* (1952). Hemingway was a sometimes combative, brawling embodiment of "the man's man," and his books have inspired both condemnation and imitation, irritation and admiration. His own adventures often embodied those of his heroes, who lived as loners, following their own code of ethics, doomed to defeat. Hemingway's deceptively simple writing style is considered to be his most important contribution to American literature. He concentrated on understatement, finding exactly the right words to use, omitting all but the most essential. His novels and stories remain standard reading in high school and college classes.

# The Writer's Life

Ernest Miller Hemingway was born in Oak Park, Illinois, a suburb of Chicago, on July 21, 1899. He was the first son and second child of Dr. Clarence Edmonds Hemingway, an obstetrician, and Grace Hall Hemingway. He had three sisters and a brother.

Hemingway's father passed his love of hunting and fishing on to his children, particularly during the family's summer visits to Windermere, their cottage in northern Michigan. Hemingway's mother, a pious and domineering woman, taught music and nearly fashioned a career as an operatic singer.

**Boyhood.** Both of Hemingway's grandfathers were U.S. Civil War veterans, so he grew up amid echoes of war. Hemingway's boyhood in Oak Park and northern Michigan appears to have been happy. Although he was not especially adept, he lettered in football and made the varsity swimming team in high school. Despite his weak eyesight, he excelled in the Boy's Rifle Club. He became an accomplished boxer, and, more important, he wrote for the school newspaper and placed three stories in *Tabula*, the school literary magazine.

**Journalist and Soldier.** Hemingway did not go to college but took a job with the *Kansas City Star* in 1917, where he covered the police beat for six months, emerging from the experience aware of the darker aspects of life. Hemingway was eager to experience combat after the United States entered World War I in April 1917, but his near-sightedness kept him out of military service. However, with a fellow reporter he joined the Italian Red Cross am-

Hemingway (center) with his little sister and his friend around 1904.

This oval-framed photograph of Hemingway appeared in his high school yearbook in 1917.

bulance service, and by June 1918 he was at the front in northern Italy. On July 8 he was seriously wounded in the leg during an artillery barrage that killed one soldier and injured another, whom he helped back to the aid station. Hemingway was decorated for bravery. After the war he worked as a reporter for the *Toronto Star* in Canada and continued to write stories.

**First Marriage and Paris.** In October 1920 Hemingway met Hadley Richardson. He married her on September 3, 1921, and they soon left for Paris, where Hemingway committed himself to the writer's life. He carried a letter from one of the leading fiction writers of the day, Sherwood Anderson, introducing him to such American expatriate writers as Ezra Pound and Gertrude Stein, who had dubbed the group the "lost generation." The Hemingways lived on Hadley's trust fund and Hemingway's earnings

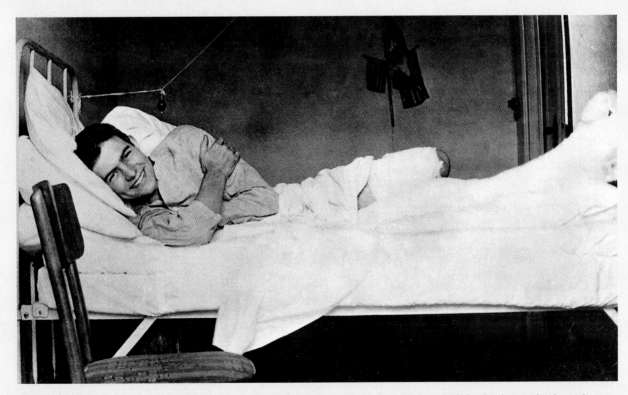

Hemingway recuperates in bed at the Red Cross Hospital in Milan, Italy, in the summer of 1918, after he received a serious wound to his leg on the front in northern Italy during World War I.

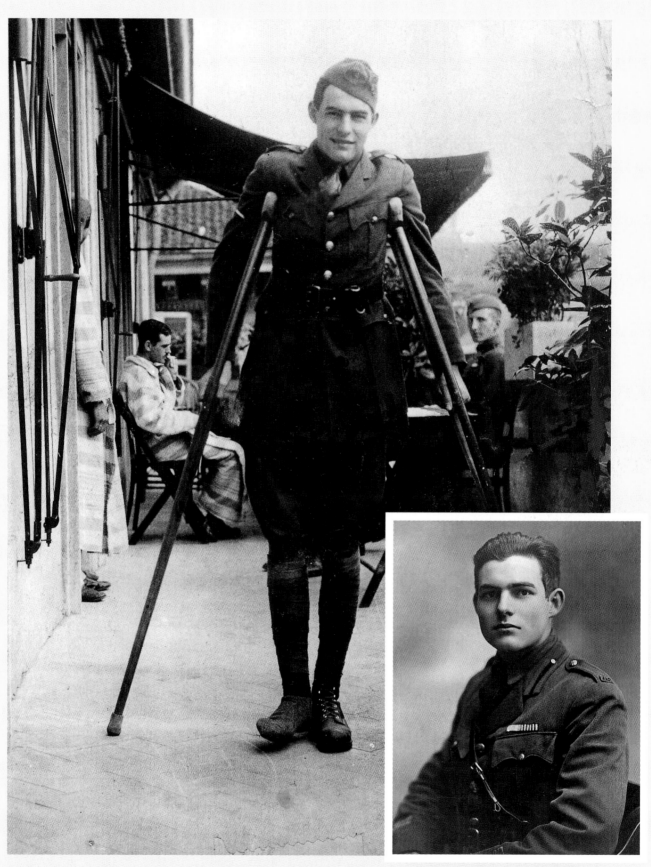

Back on his feet again, nineteen-year-old Hemingway gets around with the aid of crutches at the Red Cross Hospital in Milan, Italy, in 1918. Inset: Hemingway poses for a formal portrait in full uniform. Much of Hemingway's writing reflects his experiences as an ambulance driver during World War I and his time as a war correspondent during the Spanish Civil War and World War II.

as a correspondent for the *Toronto Star*. They had money problems, but they were not as poor as Hemingway later implied in his memoir, *A Moveable Feast* (1964).

John Hadley (Bumby), Hemingway's first son, was born in 1923. Two years later, Hemingway published his first important book, a collection of stories entitled *In Our Time*. The somewhat autobiographical protagonist, Nick Adams, appears in several stories, including "Big Two-Hearted River."

Following the publication of a satiric novella, *Torrents of Spring* (1926), Hemingway wrote one of his most important novels, *The Sun Also Rises* (1926), which takes place in Paris and Pamplona, Spain, where disillu-

sioned expatriates make love, quarrel, drink, and watch the bullfights. The next year Hemingway turned out a book of short fiction, *Men Without Women*, which includes "Hills Like White Elephants" and "The Killers." Later that year he and Hadley divorced, and he married Pauline Pfeiffer, fashion editor for the Paris edition of *Vogue*.

**Key West, Africa, and Spain.** In 1928 Hemingway and Pauline moved to Key West, which was to be their home for about ten years. Later that year, Hemingway's son Patrick was born, and Hemingway's father killed himself with a revolver. In 1929, at the age of thirty, Hemingway secured his reputation with the publication of his powerful novel of war and romance, *A Farewell to Arms*. His third son, Gregory Hancock, was born in 1931. In 1932 Hemingway published his first book of nonfiction, *Death in the Afternoon*, a commentary on the aesthetics of bullfighting. Also produced in 1932 was the first of many films to be based on his writings, *A Farewell to Arms*, starring Gary Cooper and Helen Hayes. Generally, Hemingway disliked Hollywood versions of his fiction but recognized that they contributed immensely to his prosperity and popularity.

*Winner Take Nothing*, a short fiction collection that includes "A Clean, Well-Lighted Place" and "The Gambler, the Nun, and the Radio," appeared in 1933. These stories reflect the pessimism of the Great Depression of the 1930s, which followed the collapse of the stock market in 1929. With the financial backing of Pauline's uncle, Hemingway and his wife went on safari to Africa, where he was to set two of his most famous stories, "The Short Happy Life of Francis Macomber" and "The Snows of Kilimanjaro." The most immediate result of the safari, however, was a "slightly fictionalized" account of his adventures, *Green Hills of Africa* (1935).

In 1937 Hemingway worked as a correspondent during the Spanish Civil War, which provided him with material for several stories, his only full-length play, *The Fifth Column* (1938), and the novel *For Whom the Bell Tolls* (1940). He also published *To Have and Have Not*

Hemingway poses with bookstore owner Sylvia Beach in front of her bookstore, Shakespeare and Company, in Paris in 1928. Beach's bookstore became a popular gathering spot for the "lost generation," a term used to describe Americans writing and living abroad.

(1937), a novel concerning the human costs of the depression. In 1938 Scribner's published *The Fifth Column and the First Forty-nine Stories*, which included the play, the stories from his earlier books, and four new stories, including the two set in Africa.

**Cuba and World War II.** One casualty of the Spanish Civil War was Hemingway's marriage to Pauline. While in Madrid, he met fellow writer Martha Gellhorn, and after he separated from Pauline, he and Martha moved to Finca Vigia (Lookout Farm) near Havana, Cuba. They married in 1940, the year *For Whom the Bell Tolls* was published.

In 1942 Hemingway outfitted his fishing boat, *Pilar*, to hunt for German submarines in the Caribbean, but without success. In 1944 he followed Martha to Europe and served as a war correspondent, flying with the British Royal Air Force on bombing missions. In England he met a newswoman, Mary Welsh, whom he married in 1946 after divorcing his third wife. He remained married to Mary until his death in 1961.

**Ending in Idaho.** During the last fifteen years of his life, Hemingway divided his time between Cuba and Ketchum, Idaho, where he enjoyed fishing and hunting. He wrote drafts of an epic adventure novel, the memoir of his early days in Paris, a second book about bullfighting, a second book about an African safari, and a novel of gender intrigue, which was edited heavily and published posthumously as *The Garden of Eden* in 1986. His 1950 romance novel, *Across the River and into the Trees*, is set in Venice and involves a dying colonel and a young Italian woman. The novel was assailed by critics, who claimed that Papa, as he liked his friends to call him, had lost it. However, two years later, Hemingway's remarkable novella, *The Old Man and the Sea*, won him both a Pulitzer Prize (1953) and a Nobel Prize in literature (1954).

Hemingway and Mary visited Africa on safari in 1953, but with disastrous results. They experienced two plane crashes and were mistakenly reported dead after the first. In his last years, Hemingway's injuries, combined with his blood pressure, chronic depression, and other ailments as well as years of heavy drinking, began to take their toll. Despite his sizable income from book, film, and television rights, he grew paranoid about his finances, believing that the FBI was investigating him. Subjection to shock therapy deepened his distress. Yielding to his fascination with suicide, Hemingway killed himself with his shotgun on July 2, 1961, at his home in Ketchum.

**The Aftermath.** Ernest Hemingway achieved legendary status in his lifetime, and his face was almost as familiar as those of movie stars. He left several manuscripts in various stages of completion, all of which were printed in edited form. The most nearly complete book, *A Moveable Feast*, appeared in 1964, followed by *Islands in the Stream* (1970), *The Dangerous Summer* (1985), and *The Garden of Eden*. *True at First Light* was published in 1999, on the centennial of his birth.

Hemingway in France in the 1940s. Although essentially a newsman during World War II, Hemingway impressed many professional soldiers with his bravery and his expertise in military matters.

# HIGHLIGHTS IN HEMINGWAY'S LIFE

**1899**  Ernest Miller Hemingway is born on July 21 in Oak Park, Illinois.

**1917**  Graduates from Oak Park High School; works as reporter for *Kansas City Star*.

**1918**  Serves as Red Cross ambulance driver in Italy; is badly wounded.

**1921**  Marries Hadley Richardson; moves to Paris.

**1923**  First son, John Hadley, is born.

**1925**  Publishes full-length book of short stories, *In Our Time*.

**1926**  Publishes first important novel, *The Sun Also Rises*.

**1927**  Divorced by Hadley; marries Pauline Pfeiffer.

**1928**  Moves to Key West; second son, Patrick, is born; father commits suicide.

**1929**  Publishes novel *A Farewell to Arms*, which becomes his first major commercial success.

**1931**  Third son, Gregory Hancock, is born.

**1933**  Goes on African safari with Pauline.

**1937**  Works as war correspondent in Spanish Civil War.

**1938**  Publishes *The Fifth Column and the First Forty-nine Stories*.

**1939**  Separates from Pauline; moves to Cuba.

**1940**  Marries Martha Gellhorn; publishes *For Whom the Bell Tolls*.

**1944**  Works as war correspondent in Europe.

**1945**  Divorced by Martha.

**1946**  Marries Mary Welsh; lives in Cuba and Ketchum, Idaho.

**1952**  Publishes novella *The Old Man and the Sea*, which wins a Pulitzer Prize.

**1953**  Goes on second African safari.

**1954**  Injured in two plane crashes in Africa; is awarded Nobel Prize in literature.

**1961**  Commits suicide in Ketchum on July 2.

**1964**  *A Moveable Feast*, a Paris memoir, is published posthumously.

**1986**  Posthumous novel, *The Garden of Eden*, is published.

**1989**  U.S. Postal Service issues Hemingway commemorative stamp.

**1999**  The last posthumous book, *True at First Light*, is published.

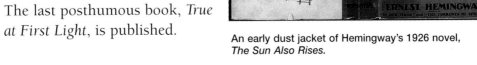

An early dust jacket of Hemingway's 1926 novel, *The Sun Also Rises*.

# The Writer's Work

Ernest Hemingway wrote occasional poems and two plays, but most of his work is fiction or nonfiction. Most readers prefer his fiction but are divided in their preferences between the stories and the novels. No serious American writer has shown comparable scope with respect to place, which is what some of Hemingway's best fiction is about as much as it is about war or love. His early fiction focuses on the theme of painful initiation into the harsh realities of life. Much of his fiction concerns men and women in love and under so much pressure that their relationships are pushed to the limit.

**Places in Hemingway's Fiction.** Ernest Hemingway was a cosmopolite, a citizen of the world who lived and traveled all over the globe. In his youth, he lived in Chicago, northern Michigan, and Kansas City. He spent time in Italy, especially Milan and Venice, during both World War I and World War II; he lived in Paris in the 1920s. He spent much time in Spain, from the bullfights of the 1920s to the agony of the Spanish Civil War in the 1930s and back to the bullfights in the summer of 1959. He went on safari in Africa in both 1933 and 1953. He had a home in Key West for

Regina McFadden's 1999 oil painting *Pinar del Río*, named for a province in western Cuba, captures the fiery orange landscape that would have been familiar scenery to Hemingway during his years in Cuba.

Hemingway, a prolific writer, was never far from pen and paper. Here, he writes while he relaxes at his home outside of Havana, Cuba, in 1948.

about ten years starting in 1928 and a home in Cuba for almost twenty years starting in 1939. In 1941 he accompanied his third wife, Martha, on a visit to China to cover the Sino-Japanese War. Beginning with occasional visits in 1930, he spent the last years of his life as a resident of Ketchum, near Sun Valley, Idaho.

Hemingway could speak several languages, particularly Italian, French, and Spanish, and was at home nearly everywhere. Although several of his stories, such as "Big Two-Hearted River," are set in America, the settings of twelve of his books are located abroad.

## Initiation Theme.

Hemingway often focuses on the coming-of-age ritual, which concerns a boy or young man whose ideals are threatened by painful realities that doom him to defeat. This loss of innocence is first seen in his early Nick Adams stories, such as "Indian Camp" and "The Battler," and culminates in the general disillusionment of the characters in *The Sun Also Rises*. Throughout Hemingway's work is the evolution of the so-called code hero, who learns to deal with fear, death, and despair by holding tightly to himself. This hero has been wounded either physically or psychologically but resists breaking under the pressure by living according to careful, self-prescribed rituals of the sort described in "Big Two-Hearted River." For Hemingway, part of the appeal of bullfighting, as described in *Death in the Afternoon*, is its highly ritualistic nature.

## Romance Under Pressure.

Hemingway wrote to F. Scott Fitzgerald in 1926 that courage is "grace under pressure." He might have said the same for love, because in most of his works, the lovers struggle against overwhelming odds. Both *A Farewell to Arms* and *For Whom the Bell Tolls* are set during wartime. In *The Sun Also Rises*, Jake Barnes's love for Brett Ashley is thwarted by several things: his sexual impotence from an undisclosed war injury; Brett's promiscuity owing to her frustration with Jake's limitations; and Robert Cohn's refusal to obey Jake's codes and rituals. Some of Hemingway's most powerful stories, such as "A

Very Short Story" and "The Short Happy Life of Francis Macomber," concern the failure of love.

## The Hemingway Style.

Although Hemingway occasionally wrote sentences that were more than two hundred words long, the typical Hemingway sentence is described by such words as "terse" and "bulletlike." He often employs a variety of polysyndeton—a frequent use of conjunctions, most notably "and"—linking elements in a sentence together in a way that implies all parts are of equal importance, while in fact one unit of the series may be much more significant than the others. Hemingway was a master of realistic colloquial speech, and because they contain so much dialogue, his stories often read like plays. Hemingway's descriptions are always exact and frequently memorable, but they are rarely lush or vividly pictorial. One of his favorite devices is omission, or what he called the "iceberg principle," whereby he holds back all details but those that are absolutely essential in conveying his point. The most famous example occurs in "Hills Like White Elephants," in which neither character mentions the difficult topic under discussion—abortion.

## BIBLIOGRAPHY

Baker, Carlos. *Ernest Hemingway: A Life Story*. New York: Charles Scribner's Sons, 1969.

_____. *Hemingway: The Writer as Artist*. 4th ed. Princeton, N.J.: Princeton University Press, 1972.

Donaldson, Scott. *By Force of Will: The Life and Art of Ernest Hemingway*. New York: Viking, 1977.

Kert, Bernice. *The Hemingway Women*. New York: W. W. Norton, 1983.

Lynn, Kenneth S. *Hemingway*. New York: Fawcett Columbine, 1987.

Oliver, Charles M. *Ernest Hemingway A to Z*. New York: Checkmark Books, 1999.

Reynolds, Michael. *Hemingway: The Final Years*. New York: W. W. Norton, 1999.

_____. *Hemingway: The Homecoming*. Oxford, England: Blackwell, 1992.

*Hemingway: The 1930s*. New York: W. W. Norton, 1997.

Smith, Paul. *A Reader's Guide to the Short Stories of Ernest Hemingway*. Boston: G. K. Hall, 1989.

# SOME INSPIRATIONS BEHIND HEMINGWAY'S WORK

Hemingway was a man of action who believed that to see death close up, which he first did as a reporter for the *Kansas City Star*, was essential to a writer. He read extensively in military history and wrote often about war, but he frequently expressed his hatred of it. Nevertheless, he experienced firsthand action in World War I (1918), the Greco-Turkish War (1922), the Spanish Civil War (1937), the Sino-Japanese War (1941), and World War II (1942–1945), not to mention sporadic revolutions in Cuba. Throughout his life he was attracted to blood sports. He loved fishing, hunting, boxing, cockfights, and bullfights. He was highly competitive and admired both toughness and courage. For Hemingway, the vital distinction between war and blood sports was that war is uncontrollable. He maintained that a bullfight could and *should* be art but that a battle could never be art.

Various writers and artists also influenced Hemingway, especially early in his career. His early training at the *Kansas City Star* helped him to hone his vigorous prose, lean sentences, and short paragraphs. He was influenced by both the realist fiction of Sherwood Anderson and the experimental techniques of Gertrude Stein. His friend the novelist F. Scott Fitzgerald helped him with the ending of *The Sun Also Rises*. Fitzgerald also connected Hemingway with Scribner's, which became his publisher, and with Maxwell Perkins, the most famous editor of that era.

Despite assertions that his characters were entirely fictitious, Hemingway frequently drew from his own life to create his fiction. The character of Nick Adams does not equal Ernest Hemingway, but they do have much in common. In more than one story, Nick broods over his father's suicide and reflects on a mother who is similar to Grace Hemingway. Like most writers, Hemingway was influenced by experiences, both his own and those of others he knew or heard about. His protagonists, almost always male, often share his personality traits, interests, and attitudes.

The quintessential outdoors man, Hemingway was an avid hunter and fisherman. Here, he proudly displays his catch of rainbow trout in Sun Valley, Idaho, in October of 1939. A few years later, in September of 1942, he was joined by actor Gary Cooper (center) for a bird shoot in Sun Valley. The gentleman on the right is their tour guide, Taylor Williams.

# Hemingway's Posthumously Published Books

Probably no other writer has had as many "new" books published after his death as Ernest Hemingway. However, the posthumous publication of his drafts has occasioned considerable debate. Some critics and scholars question whether the incomplete works should have been released at all, and many argue that the posthumous books, both fiction and nonfiction, add little luster to Hemingway's reputation. The theme of loss dominates these books.

Philip Young, an editor and scholar, published a collectin of Hemingway's stories and incomplete works as *The Nick Adams Stories* in 1972, eleven years after the author's death. The collection has been criticized as the kind of opportunism that Hemingway would have despised. Other books, notably *True at First Light* (1999), which is presumably the last that will be published because it was saved for the centennial year of Hemingway's birth, were heavily edited.

**A Moveable Feast (1964).** Hemingway's memoir of his and his first wife Hadley's experience in Paris in the 1920's is the least controversial of the posthumous works, because it was essentially complete when Hemingway killed himself. It appears that he withheld the book from publication only because he was concerned about offending people who were still alive at the time. The title refers to feast days in a church calendar that occur every year on the same days of the week but on variable dates such as Easter or Thanksgiving. In the epigraph, Hemingway describes Paris as "a moveable feast." It is a phrase he used often.

In the twenty essays that constitute *A Moveable Feast*, Hemingway describes Paris in loving and often charming detail, and he reflects on the genteel poverty that he and Hadley endured as he found his way as a writer. The book is notable, and sometimes notorious, for its portraits of such famous lost generation writers as Gertrude Stein, Ezra Pound, F. Scott Fitzgerald, Ford Madox Ford, and Wyndham Lewis. The memoir also outlines the disintegration of Hemingway's first marriage, about which he was always to have regrets.

**Islands in the Stream (1970).** The longest of Hemingway's novels, *Islands in the Stream* was to have been a section of an epic three-part novel of sea, land, and air. The land and air novels were never written. Extensively cut, the novel is fragmented and somewhat sprawling in nature. The main character is a divorced painter, Thomas Hudson, who fishes for sharks and swordfish off small islands in the Bahamas with his three sons in the summer of 1935 in part 1, "Bimini." At the end of that part Hudson receives news that two of his sons have been killed in an auto accident in France.

In part 2, "Cuba," Hudson operates his fishing boat as a World War II German submarine chaser in 1944 and drinks heavily to forget the death of his third son, who has been killed in action in France. In part 3, "At Sea," Hudson pursues a German submarine and is mortally wounded. Although, like Robert Jordan in *For Whom the Bell Tolls* (1940), Hudson lives up to the code of "grace under pressure," he is a lonely man and a failure as an artist.

**The Dangerous Summer (1985).** A newly edited version of a nonfiction book on bullfighting, *The Dangerous Summer* appeared in 1985, but it is fairly close to the version serialized in *Life* magazine in 1959, so its status as a posthumous work is debatable.

**The Garden of Eden (1986).** Hemingway's ninth and last novel, *The Garden of Eden*, the most controversial of his posthumous works, was cut to about one-third of its original manuscript length. It is set on the French Riviera in the 1920's and involves "gender intrigue," as a young American writer, David Bourne, and his beautiful wife, Catherine, both fall in love with the same woman, Marita, who is a lesbian. David and Catherine have been indulging in erotic role-switching; Catherine cuts her hair short like a boy and calls herself "Peter." Catherine urges Marita to make love to her husband, and the triangle is complete.

Meanwhile, David writes a book about elephant hunting with his father in Africa, and that narrative is woven into the latter pages of *The Garden of Eden*. At the end of the novel Catherine, realizing she no longer belongs, vindictively burns David's manuscripts and leaves their "Garden of Eden" to Marita and David, who begins to rewrite his African story. When Catherine leaves, David's potency as both lover and writer returns. This novel caused extensive reconsideration of Hemingway's treatment of female characters and examination of the theme of androgyny throughout his writings.

**True at First Light (1999).** This "fictional memoir" is an account of Hemingway's safari in 1953 with his fourth wife, Mary, which ended in a pair of near-fatal airplane crashes. Neither crash is recounted, although frequent reference is made to flights in and out of camp. Some readers might assume that the crashes are significantly omitted in the narrative. Hemingway's second son, Patrick, trimmed the eight-hundred-page manuscript considerably and edited the text heavily, but apparently not excessively. Much of the action is devoted to the project of Mary's shooting her first lion, but in the dominant plot Mary struggles with Ernest, who is trying to figure out how to accomplish a second, bigamous marriage with Debba, a tribal girl about one-third his age. The book bears comparison, and especially contrast, to *Green Hills of Africa* (1935), Hemingway's account of his 1933 safari with his second wife, Pauline, which Hemingway described as a novel in which "none of the characters or incidents . . . is imaginary."

## A FAREWELL TO ARMS

**Genre:** Novel
**Subgenre:** Wartime romance
**Published:** New York, 1929
**Time period:** 1915–1918
**Setting:** Northern Italy; Switzerland

**Themes and Issues.** The title of this novel is a pun. The "arms" represent both the arms of one's beloved, whom one leaves when going off to war, and the weapons of war, which the protagonist, Frederic Henry, ultimately puts aside in order to join his beloved, Catherine Barkley, a British nurse, late in the novel. The bitter irony is that by the end of the novel, Henry has bid farewell to arms in both senses. Whereas genuine love appeared to be impossible in the postwar world of *The Sun Also Rises*, here it happens during the war itself, another irony, in that war is a grand-scale testament to the failure of the principles of love. At one point Catherine tells Henry, "There isn't any me," a self-abnegating assertion that signifies true love. *A Farewell to Arms* makes a powerful statement against war, which destroys love and life itself.

**The Plot.** The first-person protagonist, Lieutenant Frederic Henry, is an American volunteer in the Italian Red Cross ambulance ser-

A still from the 1932 motion picture *A Farewell to Arms*, the film version of Hemingway's classic 1929 tale of love and war. Like the novel's protagonist, Hemingway himself fell in love with a nurse while recovering from a leg injury in Milan.

vice. The first two chapters hurry through the years 1915 and 1916, and when Frederic meets Catherine, whose fiancé was killed earlier in the war, it is 1917. Although Catherine initially resists, she and Frederic soon become lovers.

Frederic is wounded in the leg, and as he recovers in a Milan hospital, Catherine reappears, and they resume their relationship. When she reveals that she is pregnant, Frederic admits he feels "trapped," but their love survives. When the head nurse discovers bottles of brandy Frederic has hidden, she cancels his leave and he is again sent to the front. He arrives in late October 1917, in time for the Battle of Caporetto, a disaster for the Italians. In the panic of the Italian retreat, the

A poster promoting the 1943 film adaptation of Hemingway's *For Whom the Bell Tolls.*

## FILMS BASED ON HEMINGWAY'S STORIES

1932  *A Farewell to Arms*
1943  *For Whom the Bell Tolls*
1944  *To Have and Have Not*
1946  *The Killers*
1947  *The Macomber Affair*
1950  *The Breaking Point*
1950  *Under My Skin*
1952  *The Snows of Kilimanjaro*
1952  *Fifty Grand* (TV)
1955  *The Battler* (TV)
1955  *A Farewell to Arms* (TV)
1957  *The Sun Also Rises*
1957  *To Have and Have Not* (TV)
1957  *The World of Nick Adams* (TV)
1958  *A Farewell to Arms*
1958  *Fifty Grand*
1958  *The Old Man and the Sea*
1958  *The Gun Runners* (TV)
1959  *For Whom the Bell Tolls* (TV)
1959  *The Gambler, the Nun, and the Radio* (TV)
1959  *The Fifth Column* (TV)
1959  *The Killers* (TV)
1959  *The Snows of Kilimanjaro* (TV)
1962  *Hemingway's Adventures of a Young Man*
1962  *The Battler*
1964  *The Killers*
1977  *Islands in the Stream*
1979  *My Old Man* (TV)
1984  *The Sun Also Rises* (TV)
1990  *The Old Man and the Sea* (TV)
1997  *In Love and War*
1998  *Hills Like White Elephants* (TV)
1999  *The Old Man and the Sea*
2000  *A Moveable Feast*

## LONG FICTION

1926 The Torrents of Spring
1926 The Sun Also Rises
1929 A Farewell to Arms
1937 To Have and Have Not
1940 For Whom the Bell Tolls
1950 Across the River and
     into the Trees
1952 The Old Man and the
     Sea
1970 Islands in the Stream
1986 The Garden of Eden

## PLAYS

1926 Today Is Friday
1938 The Fifth Column

## SHORT FICTION

1923 Three Stories and Ten
     Poems
1925 In Our Time
1927 Men Without Women
1933 Winner Take Nothing
1938 The Fifth Column and
     the First Forty-nine
     Stories
1961 The Snows of
     Kilimanjaro and Other
     Stories
1972 The Nick Adams Stories
1987 The Complete Short
     Stories

## NONFICTION

1932 Death in the Afternoon
1935 Green Hills of Africa
1964 A Moveable Feast
1967 By-Line: Ernest
     Hemingway, Selected
     Articles, and Dispatches
     of Four Decades
1981 Ernest Hemingway:
     Selected Letters,
     1917–1961
1985 The Dangerous Summer
1985 Dateline, Toronto: The
     Complete "Toronto Star"
     Dispatches, 1920–1924
1999 True at First Light

military police seize officers at random and shoot them as infiltrators. After witnessing one such execution, Frederic escapes by leaping into a river.

By the time he again reaches Milan, Frederic has decided to desert the service. He finds Catherine at a hospital on Lake Maggiore. When the barman at their hotel warns him that the authorities are on the way, Frederic and Catherine row a boat across the lake to sanctuary in Switzerland. They spend an idyllic winter in a mountain chalet, but Catherine experiences complications delivering her baby, which is stillborn. Catherine dies soon afterward, leaving Frederic alone and disconsolate.

**Analysis.** Ernest Hemingway's symbolic use of setting is apparent from the opening pages, in which dust rises as troops march over the ground and dry leaves fall as autumn approaches. Rain plays a significant role in setting the mood. With winter and "permanent rain," conditions change for the worse, and cholera strikes. Catherine has an unusual fear of rain. It rains when Frederic makes his escape from the execution site. It rains again when Frederic and Catherine row toward Switzerland and, finally, on the evening of Catherine's death.

Although Frederic never appears to be altogether idealistic, he presumably volunteers for service believing that he can make a difference. He learns, however, that "words such as glory, honor, courage, or hallow" are "obscene." Through this bitter wisdom Frederic experiences the painful initiation ritual that nearly all Hemingway's protagonists must endure. When Frederic shoots billiards with Count Greffi late in the novel, he speculates on the wisdom of age, but the old man informs him he has arrived not at wisdom but rather at cynicism.

## SOURCES FOR FURTHER STUDY

Bloom, Harold, ed. *Modern Critical Interpretations: Ernest Hemingway's "A Farewell to Arms."* New York: Chelsea House, 1987.

Donaldson, Scott, ed. *New Essays on "A Farewell to Arms."* Cambridge, England: Cambridge University Press, 1990.

Lewis, Robert W. *"A Farewell to Arms": The War of the Words.* Boston: Twayne Publishers, 1991.

Reynolds, Michael. *Hemingway's First War: The Making of "A Farewell to Arms."* Princeton, N.J.: Princeton University Press, 1976.

Spilka, Mark. *Hemingway's Quarrel with Androgyny.* Lincoln: University of Nebraska Press, 1990.

## FOR WHOM THE BELL TOLLS

**Genre:** Novel
**Subgenre:** Wartime romance
**Published:** New York, 1940
**Time period:** 1937
**Setting:** Guadarrama Mountains, Spain

**Themes and Issues.** In this novel, as in *A Farewell to Arms*, true love in time of war is possible, but it cannot survive. Here, however, the message is more affirmative, even though the protagonist, Robert Jordan, dies at the end. Despite Jordan's setbacks, he avoids yielding to cynicism. He is content in the knowledge that he has fought for his beliefs and that, in helping his beloved Maria to escape, part of him will stay alive in her. Jordan seems to wear qualities such as glory and honor more comfortably than other Hemingway heroes, such as Jake Barnes or Frederic Henry. While all three protagonists could be described as courageous, only Jordan appears capable of an altruism that neither of the others possesses.

As Hemingway demonstrates, the Spanish Civil War was marked by unprecedented atrocities on both sides. Hemingway, who was fiercely antifascist, makes clear his own commitment to the Republican, or Loyalist, cause. *For Whom the Bell Tolls* is his most overtly political novel, and his sympathy for leftist ideology is obvious.

Mark Tansey's 1986 oil painting *Forward Retreat* gives the illusion of traveling backward and forward in an upside-down world. While Robert Jordan of Hemingway's *For Whom the Bell Tolls* ultimately loses his life during the Spanish Civil War, he makes great strides in defending his cause and the people he loves.

**The Plot.** Robert Jordan, a Spanish instructor on leave from the University of Montana, has come to Spain as a demolition expert to blow up a bridge over which the Fascists plan to attack. He meets a band of partisans in the mountains, led by the suspicious Pablo, whose earlier courage has evaporated, leaving him a drunken coward who is not interested in the bridge, only in maintaining his safe hideout. Pablo's forty-eight-year-old wife, Pilar, a peasant woman of great strength and courage, is the real leader of the band.

Jordan meets the beautiful, blond Maria, and they fall in love at first sight. Three months earlier, Maria had been forced to watch her parents being gunned down by the Fascists. She was then gang raped, and her head was shaved. Pilar, Maria's surrogate mother figure, believes that love will cure Maria's trauma, and she promotes the romance, which kindles quickly.

From the outset Jordan senses a "sadness" in Pablo that he believes will lead Pablo to betrayal. Moreover, early in the novel, when Pilar reads Pablo's palm, she refuses to say what she sees, making it obvious that he is doomed. As the critical moment approaches, Pablo steals the detonator needed to blow up the bridge. Tension is maintained by delaying the climactic action with flashbacks and scene shifts. Jordan, for example, recalls the party atmosphere at the headquarters in Madrid and reflects bitterly on his father's suicide. When Jordan sends Andres to warn General Golz, a Loyalist, of an impending attack, action shifts between Andres's mission and that of Jordan.

As the novel closes, Andres delivers his message, but it is too late. Jordan manages to blow up the bridge without a detonator, but the loyal old man of the partisans, Anselmo, is killed, and in the retreat a Fascist tank cuts down Jordan's horse and injures his leg. The novel ends with Jordan, injured and dying, firing a machine gun to cover the retreat of the partisans.

**Analysis.** The novel's action covers only three days, but flashbacks and digressions give it a broader scope. In fact, this novel might be called an epic of modern Spain, and it is surely Hemingway's love song to the Spanish people, about whom Jordan reflects, "There is no people like them when they are good and when they go bad there is no people that is worse." Hemingway's view of the Spanish, as of all the nationalities and ethnic groups he wrote about, was never blindly complimentary. Throughout the text he scatters Spanish words and phrases, and the characters use the intimate "thee" and "thou" form of address, as if they were actually speaking Spanish. The impact of this technique is illustrated in a passage in which Jordan tells Maria of his love: "I love thee as I love all that we have fought for. I love thee as I love liberty and dignity and the rights of all men to work and not be hungry. I love thee as I love Madrid that we have defended and as I love all my comrades that have died."

Although *For Whom the Bell Tolls* was the unanimous choice of the panel for the Pulitzer Prize in letters in 1941, the chair overturned the recommendation on the grounds that it was too controversial. No Pulitzer Prize for fiction was awarded that year.

## SOURCES FOR FURTHER STUDY

Broer, Lawrence R. *Hemingway's Spanish Tragedy.* Tuscaloosa: University of Alabama Press, 1973.

Grebstein, Sheldon Norman, ed. *Merrill Studies in "For Whom the Bell Tolls."* Columbus, Ohio: Charles E. Merrill, 1971.

Josephs, Allen. *"For Whom the Bell Tolls": Ernest Hemingway's Undiscovered Country.* New York: Twayne Publishers, 1994.

Sanderson, Rena, ed. *Blowing the Bridge: Essays on Hemingway and "For Whom the Bell Tolls."* New York: Greenwood Press, 1992.

Wirt, William. *The Tragic Art of Ernest Hemingway.* Baton Rouge: Louisiana State University Press, 1981.

## THE SUN ALSO RISES
   **Genre:** Novel
   **Subgenre:** Romance
   **Published:** New York, 1926
   **Time period:** 1920s
   **Setting:** Paris, France; Pamplona, Spain

**Themes and Issues.** Hemingway's best-known novel, *The Sun Also Rises*, deals with

The characters of Hemingway's novel *The Sun Also Rises* find temporary relief from the mundaneness of postwar Europe in their social gatherings. Here, from left to right are actors Eddie Albert (Bill Gorton), Errol Flynn (Mike Campbell), Mel Ferrer (Robert Cohn), Tyrone Power (Jake Barnes), and Ava Gardner (Lady Brett) in a still from the 1957 film adaptation of the novel.

the spiritual alienation of American expatriates in Europe following World War I. Hemingway implies that isolationist America, with its prohibition against liquor, is culturally backward and dull. Europe, with the parties of Paris and the bullfights of Pamplona, appears to offer more escape than real consolation. Hemingway depicts postwar Europe as a wasteland, in which love is impossible and lovemaking is meaningless. The novel's title, combined with introductory quotations from Gertrude Stein and the biblical Book of Ecclesiastes, suggests not only a sense of loss but also a frustrating, inescapable cycle. The relief offered by the atmosphere of the fiesta and the ritual of the bullfights is illusory. What redeems the situation and makes the novel a tragedy is Jake Barnes's courageous refusal to submit to his own or society's limitations.

**The Plot.** In Paris the first-person protagonist, Jake Barnes, a journalist whose war injury has left him impotent, copes with his doomed love for Lady Brett Ashley. Brett is a war widow who loves Jake but is frustrated with his inability to consummate their passion. The antagonist, Robert Cohn, a former boxing champion at Princeton, rejects his fiancé and runs off with Brett.

In book 2, which contains the novel's central action, Jake and two friends, one of whom is Mike Campbell, Brett's fiancé from Scotland, go fishing in northern Spain. Jake's depression over Brett's affair with Cohn partially lifts, but his hard feelings flare up again in Pamplona, where they all go to watch the running of the bulls. Jake is an aficionado of bullfighting and possesses a deep love and understanding of its traditions and rituals. Cohn, however, remains an outsider who understands little about bullfighting, is unable to control his drinking, and bullies others when he does not get things that he wants, such as Brett's love and respect.

Presumably to get back at Cohn, Jake introduces Brett to the bullfighter Pedro Romero. Cohn, in response, beats up both Jake and Mike then finds Brett and Romero in a hotel and attacks Romero, who refuses to hit him back. Cohn then disappears, not to be seen again. Despite his injuries, Romero fights beautifully the next day, but as the fiesta ends, Jake and his friends feel empty.

In the brief book 3, Jake parts with his friends then receives a telegram from Brett in Madrid, where she has gone with Romero, asking him to come to her rescue. At the end, although it is obvious that she still loves Jake, Brett resolves to return to her fiancé, Mike. When Brett suggests that she and Jake could have had a "good time together," Jake can only respond sardonically, "Isn't it pretty to think so?"

**Analysis.** While *The Sun Also Rises* was originally decried as amoral and misogynistic, it remains Hemingway's most widely read novel. Even modern readers identify with Jake's struggle in an apparently purposeless universe and with his statement "I did not care what it was all about. All I wanted to know was how to live in it." Moreover, later critics found sympathy for Brett's dilemma.

Jake and Brett cope as well as they can when faced with a world devoid of meaning. They may not be admirable characters, but they are believable, and when they find themselves powerless in love, they strive to live by a set of codes they must create for themselves.

## SOURCES FOR FURTHER STUDY

Lewis, Robert W. *Hemingway on Love.* Austin: University of Texas Press, 1965.

Nagel, James, ed. *Critical Essays on Ernest Hemingway's "The Sun Also Rises."* New York: G. K. Hall, 1995.

Reynolds, Michael. *Hemingway: The Paris Years.* Oxford, England: Blackwell, 1989.

Wagner-Martin, Linda, ed. *New Essays on "The Sun Also Rises."* Cambridge, England: Cambridge University Press, 1987.

Waldhorn, Arthur. *A Reader's Guide to Ernest Hemingway.* New York: Farrar, Straus and Giroux, 1972.

# *Other Works*

**THE FIFTH COLUMN AND THE FIRST FORTY-NINE STORIES** (1938). This book contains Ernest Hemingway's only full-length play, *The Fifth Column*, about counterespionage in Madrid during the Spanish Civil War, which ran for eighty-seven nights on Broadway to mixed reviews. The book also collects the contents of three earlier books of short fiction and six additional stories. Included is one of Hemingway's first stories, "Up in Michigan," which had appeared previously in a limited edition called *Three Stories & Ten Poems* (1923). The controversial story concerns the subject of what would today be called date rape.

The best two of the new stories are "The Short Happy Life of Francis Macomber" and "The Snows of Kilimanjaro," both set in Africa. In "The Short Happy Life of Francis Macomber," the title character runs from a lion he has wounded. In response, his wife, Margot, vengefully jumps into bed with a hunter, Robert Wilson, who regards American women as "the hardest, the cruelest, the most predatory and most attractive." Wilson considers American males such as Macomber to be "boy-men" who disintegrate under the pressure of such women. Macomber redeems himself, however, and changes Wilson's opinion of him when he shoots and wounds a charging buffalo. At that point Margot, apparently attempting to shoot the buffalo, misses it and kills her husband. Wilson insinuates that she has murdered Macomber because he had regained his self-confidence and would likely have left her. The ending is generally regarded as an example of intentional ambiguity.

In "The Snows of Kilimanjaro," Harry, a failed writer, is dying of gangrene while waiting for an airplane to take him to Nairobi. His wife, Helen, attempts to nurse him, but he quarrels with her as he reviews his life in a series of flashbacks pertaining to World War I and the decade following it, during which Harry divorced his first wife, drank heavily, and squandered his talent. In an epigraph, Hemingway portrays the frozen carcass of a leopard in the snow at the top of the mountain, using the leopard as a symbol for achievement. Unlike the leopard, however, Harry dies without having achieved his dreams. Some readers connect the story with Hemingway's concern over his own shortcomings as a writer.

**IN OUR TIME** (1925). This full-length collection of short fiction brings together fourteen short stories ("Big Two-Hearted River" is printed in two parts) and sixteen vignettes, originally published as *In Our Time* (1924), which he uses as interchapters. The vignettes are short journalistic pieces focusing on war, revolution, and bullfighting. The title is drawn from the Anglican Book of Common Prayer, "Give us peace in our time, O Lord." However, the time period covered by the stories is anything but peaceful.

The opening story, "Indian Camp," introduces a young Nick Adams, who witnesses a difficult Caesarean birth under primitive conditions. The husband, who cannot bear his wife's screams, commits suicide. Nick responds by insisting he will never die. In "The Battler," a somewhat older Nick encounters an addled ex-boxer and his friend, who suddenly knocks the boxer unconscious for an imaginary offense.

Nick's initiation continues through two more stories. In "Big Two-Hearted River," one of Hemingway's best, Nick appears as a veteran of World War I, attempting to gain control of his life by returning to nature. Nick carefully submits himself to the simple routines and rituals of camping and trout fishing in order to reestablish his grip on reality. Other stories, including "A Very Short Story" and "Soldier's Home," also concern men who struggle to adjust to their lives after the war.

**MEN WITHOUT WOMEN** (1927). Hemingway's second full-length collection offers fourteen stories in which women either are absent or appear only in minor roles. Implicitly, such a world would be harsh and often violent, as in the opening story, "The Undefeated," which depicts an out-of-luck bullfighter trying to maintain his dignity while being gored by a bull during a fight. "Fifty Grand," which involves prizefighting and gambling, is a sort of American counterpart to "The Undefeated."

Nick Adams reappears, although not by name, in "In Another Country" and in "The Killers," a study in fear that has been popular with filmmakers. The 1946 film version of *The Killers*, starring Burt Lancaster and Ava Gardner, was the only film based on his writings that Hemingway enjoyed. Nick Adams also appears in "Ten Indians," in which he is initiated into the pains of love, and in "Now I Lay Me," in which he is a battle-weary lieutenant in the Italian army suffering from insomnia.

One of the few stories to involve a woman significantly is "Hills Like White Elephants," in which an unnamed man tries to convince his girlfriend to have an abortion. This story is considered the classic example of Hemingway's use of omission, or what he called the "iceberg principle," whereby an important part of the story is omitted.

Hemingway's passion for bullfighting, his philosophy of grace under pressure, and his fixation with death come together in Pablo Picasso's 1933 oil painting *Corrida. Death of a Torero* (Musée Picasso, Paris, France).

**WINNER TAKE NOTHING** (1933). The title of Hemingway's third book of short stories is a commentary on the era of its publication, the Great Depression of the 1930s. Eight of the stories are set in the United States; the remaining six are set in Europe or elsewhere. The book conveys a sense of universal malaise, and it could be regarded as the most downbeat of Hemingway's story collections.

Three of the stories involve Nick Adams. In the ironically titled "The Light of the World"—as Jesus is traditionally so described—Nick is seventeen in Michigan. In "A Way You'll Never Be," he appears as a wounded soldier in Italy, fearful about his sanity. In "Fathers and Sons,"

he appears at age thirty-eight with his son. As his son sleeps, Nick reflects on his father's suicide and on his tryst with an Indian girl. These stories and twenty-one others, some of which were previously unpublished, were collected by the writer and editor Philip Young and published in 1972 as *The Nick Adams Stories*.

Several of the stories, including "God Rest You Merry, Gentlemen," "The Sea Change," and "The Mother of a Queen," concern issues of sexuality and gender identity. Here and elsewhere in his fiction Hemingway reveals his ambivalence about homosexuality, a subject to which he would return in his unfinished draft of *The Garden of Eden*.

Hemingway with his fourth wife, Mary, around 1960.

The best of the stories in this volume are "A Clean, Well-Lighted Place" and "The Gambler, The Nun, and the Radio," both of which border on nihilism. In the former, an old man who has attempted suicide tries to console himself by drinking late at night in a well-lighted café in Spain. After he leaves, the older of the two waiters recites to himself a negative version of the Lord's Prayer, which begins, "Our *nada* [nothing] who art in *nada*." In the latter story, a writer who has been injured in an automobile accident in Montana reflects on Marx's assertion that religion is "the opium of the people," concluding cynically that of the many opiates, the real one is bread.

# Resources

The most important repository of Ernest Hemingway's manuscripts is the Hemingway Collection at the John F. Kennedy Library in Boston. Other important collections are at the Ernest Hemingway Foundation in Oak Park, Illinois; the Beinecke Rare Book and Manuscript Library at Yale University; the Rare Book Room at the Alderman Library, University of Virginia; the Humanities Research Center at the University of Texas; the Library of Congress; Princeton University Library; and Stanford University Library. Other institutions and organizations of interest to students of Ernest Hemingway include the following:

**The Ernest Hemingway Foundation.** Formed on December 28, 1980, as a society with 119 individuals and 2 libraries as charter members, there are now more than 500 members in 21 countries. The society became a foundation in 1987. The foundation sponsors an international conference every two years and sessions on Hemingway at various meetings in the United States every year. The foundation sponsors *The Hemingway Review*, which evolved from *Hemingway Notes*, the first issue of which appeared in spring 1971. *The Hemingway Review* began publication in fall 1981 and is published twice a year under the auspices of the University of Idaho. The editor is Susan Beegel. Editorial offices are at 180 Polpis Road, Nantucket, MA 02554. Events are listed on (http://www.hemingway.org/EHFOP/events.html).

The foundation also publishes an eight-page *Hemingway Newsletter* in January and July.

**The Ernest Hemingway Foundation of Oak Park.** This foundation maintains Ernest Hemingway's birthplace and a museum, provides an on-line Hemingway Catalog of books, videos, and gifts and lists Web links (http://www.hemingway.org).

**The Hemingway-Pfeiffer Museum and Educational Center.** The home of Hemingway's second wife, Pauline Pfeiffer, is now a museum and educational center in Piggott, Arkansas. It is operated by Arkansas State University at Jonesboro, which provides daily tours of the home and barn that was converted into a studio for Hemingway.

**The Hemingway Home and Museum.** Hemingway's home in Key West is registered as a national historic landmark and is open to the public as a museum. Hemingway owned the property from 1931 until his death and lived there for about ten years. Nearly fifty cats, said to be descendants of Hemingway's beloved pets, roam the grounds as living memorials. The home boasts the first swimming pool built in Key West, in the late 1930s.

**The Michigan Hemingway Society.** This society presents an annual program of lectures and tours each October in Petoskey, Michigan, near where the Hemingway family's cabin, Windermere, is located. The society publishes keynote addresses at its Web site. (http://www.upnorth.net/hemingway/)

*RON MCFARLAND*

# John Hersey

**BORN:** June 17, 1914, Tianjin, China
**DIED:** March 24, 1993, Key West, Florida
**IDENTIFICATION:** Postwar novelist who based his most popular work on pressing issues of national and sometimes global significance.

John Hersey was gifted as both a journalist and a novelist, and he combined the two approaches in much of his writing. His most famous work, *Hiroshima* (1946), an account of lives before, during, and immediately after the U.S. dropping of an atom bomb in World War II, struck a nerve in its hundreds of millions of readers. Widely viewed as literature, and sometimes even as a "nonfiction novel," the book is frequently cited as the single most important piece of twentieth-century journalism. It is still assigned and read in countless classrooms. Hersey's most popular novels share *Hiroshima*'s clarity of style, choice of historically vital subject matter, and concern with the nature of personal integrity and courage. These elements ensure his continuing relevance.

Born on June 17, 1914, in Tianjin, China, John Richard Hersey was the youngest son of American Protestant missionaries Roscoe Monroe and Grace Baird Hersey. As he grew up, he spoke Chinese fluently before learning English. He was introduced to international travel at age three, going on a trip around the world with his mother, while his father was transferred as the Young Men's Christian Association (YMCA) secretary to France. At the end of their travels, mother and son returned to the Tianjin mission, where Hersey began his formal education at the Tianjin Grammar School. He later studied at the American School in Tianjin until age ten, when the family returned to the United States.

**Schooling in America.** Hersey attended his first American public schools in Briarcliff Manor, New York, from 1924 to 1927. He decided early in his life to become a journalist. From 1927 to 1932 he studied at Hotchkiss Preparatory School in Lakeville, Connecticut, and entered Yale University after graduating from high school. At Yale, he earned letters in football and wrote for the school newspaper, earning his bachelor's degree in general studies in 1936. He pursued postgraduate work at Cambridge University's Clare College in England, where he studied eighteenth-century English literature.

By this time Hersey's career interests had widened to include fiction and poetry, but he decided to aim for a position at *Time*, which he considered the liveliest magazine of its type. After graduating from Cambridge in 1937, *Time* originally rejected his request for employment. He then spent the summer working as a private secretary to the American novelist Sinclair Lewis. In the fall he was finally hired by *Time*, at the rate of thirty-five dollars a week.

**International Correspondent.** Hersey's background and the rapport he enjoyed with *Time*'s publisher, Henry Luce, helped him win an assignment in 1939 to report on developments in the Far East. There he interviewed such internationally significant figures as the Chinese Nationalist leader Chiang Kai-shek.

*Life* magazine photographer J. R. Eyerman snapped this photograph of Hersey as a young war correspondent during World War II. Hersey worked as a reporter for *Time* magazine. His experiences during the war inspired some of his most enduring works.

**First Successes.** For his first book, *Men on Bataan* (1942), Hersey drew heavily on news dispatches and engaged in some original research for his portrait of U.S. general Douglas MacArthur and the military actions on the Philippines' Bataan peninsula. In July, the month in which the book appeared, Hersey was sent to the Pacific theater as a *Time* magazine correspondent. In the fall he spent several weeks on Guadalcanal Island, where he accompanied a group of U.S. Marines led by Captain Charles Rigaud into battle. Hersey's experiences resulted in his second book, *Into the Valley: A Skirmish of the Marines* (1943).

Because of the vigor and clarity of Hersey's writing, *Into the Valley* was heralded as marking the arrival of another Ernest Hemingway. The Council of Books in Wartime called it "imperative reading for the wartime public," a distinction earned by only one book before it.

**Birth of a Novelist.** From May to September of 1943, Hersey was in the Mediterranean theater, where he accompanied U.S. invasion forces to Italy. There he found inspiration for his first novel, *A Bell for Adano* (1944), written quickly after his return to the United States. The first novel to focus on the Italian occupation, it won a wide readership. Joining Hersey's previous book as an "imperative," it was adapted for radio, theater, and film and was serialized in newspapers. In May 1945 it was awarded the Pulitzer Prize in fiction.

**Worldwide Acclaim.** In September 1945 Hersey went to China and Japan on assign-

This 1944 painting by Ben Shahn, *Italian Landscape II: Europa* (Montgomery Museum of Fine Arts, The Blount Collection, Montgomery, Alabama), captures the destruction and devastation that Hersey confronted as a war correspondent. Like Hersey, Shahn produced a number of works that commented on the devastation caused by World War II.

ment for *Life* and *The New Yorker*. It proved a productive time for him as a writer, since he was free of the editorial restrictions imposed on him as a regular correspondent. Military censorship had also ended. Hersey wrote several articles from China, then traveled on a destroyer to Japan, where he interviewed survivors of the first atom bomb, dropped on the city of Hiroshima. The resulting account, *Hiroshima*, appeared on August 31, 1946, in *The New Yorker*, which for the first time devoted an entire issue to a single feature.

A combination of journalistic techniques and fictional character development, *Hiroshima* successfully conveyed to the postwar public the still-fresh horror of the atom bombings. Its appearance in book form in October drew even greater response, in part due to the Book-of-the-Month Club, which distributed copies free to its membership. By the end of the year, the book was widely read in all major countries of the world, with the exception of Japan.

**The Established Novelist.** In 1947 Hersey turned his energies firmly toward fiction. In preparation for his second novel, he spent several years working with translators on published and unpublished materials related to the Jewish ghetto in Warsaw, Poland, and the Nazi program to exterminate Polish Jews. The resulting novel, *The Wall* (1950), won several awards, including the 1950 Daroff Award from the Jewish Book Council of America.

In 1952 Hersey became the youngest writer ever elected to the American Academy of Arts and Sciences. He played an active role in writers' organizations throughout the remainder of his career. His third novel, *The Marmot Drive*, appeared in 1953, followed in 1956 by *A Single Pebble*, his first major work to be set in the land of his birth, and in 1959 by *The War Lover*, a novel that explored the psychology of a man with a passion for death.

**Activism in Education.** Hersey was also active in efforts to improve the American educational system, becoming a member of the National Citizens Committee for the Public Schools in 1954. Other activities on behalf of local and national public education followed. He also expressed this interest in fictional form, in *The Child Buyer* (1960). In 1958 he was divorced from his first wife, Frances Ann Cannon, whom he had married in 1940. Later that year he married Barbara Day Adams Kaufman.

Leon Golub's 1960 lacquer painting *Fallen Warrior (Burnt Man)* presents a horrific vision of the effects of the atom bomb. Hersey took the lead among writers of the postwar effort to reclaim humanity. He was appalled by the bombing and spoke out against the nuclear arms race that would dominate the rest of the century.

# HIGHLIGHTS IN HERSEY'S LIFE

| | |
|---|---|
| **1914** | John Richard Hersey is born on June 17 in Tianjin, China. |
| **1924** | Family returns to the United States. |
| **1927** | Hersey enters Hotchkiss School in Connecticut. |
| **1932** | Enters Yale University. |
| **1936** | Earns bachelor's degree from Yale University; enters Cambridge University. |
| **1937** | Works as Sinclair Lewis's secretary; joins staff of *Time* magazine. |
| **1939–1945** | Serves as war correspondent for *Time* and *Life* magazines in China, the South Pacific, the Mediterranean, and Moscow. |
| **1940** | Marries Frances Ann Cannon. |
| **1942** | Publishes first nonfiction book, *Men on Bataan*. |
| **1944** | Publishes first novel, *A Bell for Adano*. |
| **1945** | Receives Pulitzer Prize in fiction for *A Bell for Adano*. |
| **1946** | Publishes *Hiroshima* in *The New Yorker* and later in book form. |
| **1950** | Publishes *The Wall*; begins fellowship at Yale University. |
| **1952** | Elected to the American Academy of Arts and Letters. |
| **1956** | Publishes *A Single Pebble*; works on Adlai Stevenson's presidential campaign staff. |
| **1958** | Divorced from Frances Cannon; marries Barbara Day Adams Kaufman. |
| **1965** | Named master of Pierson College, Yale University. |
| **1971** | Lectures at Yale. |
| **1975** | Becomes professor at Yale; elected president of Authors League of America. |
| **1985** | Publishes fortieth-anniversary edition of *Hiroshima* with new epilogue. |
| **1993** | Dies of cancer on March 24 in Key West, Florida. |

**JOHN HERSEY**

*A Bell for Adano*

WINNER OF THE PULITZER PRIZE

Throughout the 1960s, Hersey continued to write novels and published the nonfiction collection *Here to Stay: Studies in Human Tenacity* (1962), a showcase of work from his *Life* and *The New Yorker* years. The book included "A Sense of Community," his account of a crew's survival after the wreck of their patrol torpedo (PT) boat, under the command of future U.S. president Lieutenant John F. Kennedy. Hersey returned to book-length nonfiction with *The Algiers Motel Incident* (1968), a report on the 1967 rioting in Detroit.

**Educator.** Throughout the 1950s, 1960s, and 1970s, Hersey was affiliated with Yale University, beginning with a fellowship at Yale's

# SOME INSPIRATIONS BEHIND HERSEY'S WORK

When covering the Allied invasion of Italy during World War II, Hersey visited the office of the American military governor in Licata, a seaport on the southern Italian coast. His visit led directly to a dispatch, "AMGOT at Work," in *Life*, in which he told how the governor dealt with local problems. He depicted an old resident who warns about the growing black market; a cart driver accused of obstructing traffic who is brought to trial and dismissed; a wealthy householder who is awarded damages caused by careless American troops; and a young woman who is informed that her missing fiancé is alive as a prisoner of war.

At the same time, stories of the behavior of U.S. general George S. Patton, Jr., elsewhere in Italy were leaving Hersey with feelings of outrage. Patton reportedly slapped an American enlisted man and ordered a poor man's mule destroyed because its cart blocked military traffic. Spurred by his outrage, Hersey wrote *A Bell for Adano* in less than a month. The even-handed governor in Licata became Hersey's fictional Major Joppolo, while Patton became Hersey's petty General Marvin, who brings Joppolo's good-hearted rule to a sudden end.

Just as Hersey's direct experience as a reporter on Guadalcanal gave rise to *Into the Valley*, other experiences during his years as a correspondent inspired subsequent novels. His experiences and interviews while on the aircraft carrier *Hornet*, immediately before going to Guadalcanal, inspired his novel *The War Lover*, about an American pilot who lusts after death and destruction, and who has, in Hersey's view, exactly the wrong kind of courage.

During his time as a correspondent in Moscow in 1944 and 1945, Hersey had the opportunity to visit the ruins of ghettos in Warsaw, Lodz, and Tallinn, and a detention camp at Klooga, Estonia. His visits increased his knowledge of the mass killings of Jews during the war and inspired him to undertake the extensive research that led to his lengthy novel *The Wall*, about the development of underground resistance in the Warsaw ghetto.

In 1959 the Woodrow Wilson Foundation published the Hersey essay "Intelligence, Choice, and Consent." In this pamphlet, Hersey described the plight of an exceptionally bright Illinois child from a poor background, whose talent is inadequately assessed and poorly nurtured in the classroom. Many of the circumstances, problems, and analyses in the essay reappeared in his novel *The Child Buyer* the next year.

Postwar Italy offered young Hersey a wealth of images of both courage and hardship. Here, American soldiers, members of the 370th Regiment, make their way through the mountains of Prato, Italy, in April 1945.

Berkeley College in 1950. In 1965 Hersey began a five-year term as master of Pierson College. He continued to teach at Yale until his retirement in 1984. He was elected president of the Authors League of America in 1975 and served for five years. In 1985 he issued a new edition of *Hiroshima*, with a new epilogue, on the fortieth anniversary of the bombing. Hersey maintained dual residences in Martha's Vineyard, Massachusetts, and in Key West, Florida, where he died of cancer on March 24, 1993.

Although John Hersey's books appeared over more than four decades, those of the first two decades remain his best known. His fiction and nonfiction works alike are marked by a clear, journalistic writing style and the dominating influence of the work's message or moral. Both his fiction and nonfiction tend to focus on the limits and dimensions of the valor of individuals pitted against larger, often irresistible, forces.

**Issues in Hersey's Writing.** Hersey wrote on subjects that were among the most critical issues of his time. He explored the difficulties of enlightened postwar occupation in *A Bell for Adano*, the horrors of the atom-bomb explosion in *Hiroshima*, and the chilling nature of the German suppression and extermination of Jews in *The Wall*. His later novels continued to have topical interest. *The Child Buyer* focused on issues in education relating to gifted children, *White Lotus* (1965) dealt with slavery and its effects, and *My Petition for More Space* (1974) discussed the overpopulation question.

**The Character of the Observer.** Hersey's novels show an intense interest in the observer as character. Often this observer watches the action of the story from a distance, whether emotional or physical, and is moved to action only reluctantly, or even accidentally. This action, however, is often pivotal.

The engineer in *A Single Pebble*, for example, regards himself as an aloof, superior visitor to China. He realizes too late how his obser-

vations precipitate the crisis that destroys the one heroic figure of the story. The bookish archivist of *The Wall*, in contrast, is the one who preserves the heroism of those around him. He becomes heroic himself through his observation and record keeping. In *The Child Buyer*, the observers are a group of state senators holding a hearing. Although they are the most empowered characters in the novel, they are also the least active, sitting through testimonies that are necessary preludes to any actions on their part.

**The Theme of Courage.** Hersey reached his maturity as a writer during the largest and most important war of the twentieth century. As other writers before him had done, he became intensely interested in the nature of courage. "The great themes are love and death," he wrote, "their synthesis is the will to live." Old Pebble, threatened by the treacherous river in *A Single Pebble*, shows a bravery steeped in tradition, while the resistance fight-

An amputee makes his way up a long flight of stairs in Ben Shahn's 1944 painting *The Red Stairway* (The Saint Louis Art Museum, Saint Louis, Missouri). For Hersey, courage didn't necessarily manifest itself on the battlefield. It was evident in the will to endure, despite the war's lasting emotional and physical scars.

ers of *The Wall* improvise their courageous acts in the face of unprecedented dangers.

**Hersey's Literary Legacy.** Although Hersey's works were initially seen as expanding upon the tradition of novels of social responsibility, exemplified by the novels of such American authors as John Steinbeck, Hersey's greatest influence has been in the novel of contemporary history and in the so-called nonfiction novel. Hersey himself asserted that he maintained a strict division between fiction and nonfiction, assigning the higher position to fiction. Readers have continued to appreciate *Hiroshima* for its novelistic or fictional elements and *The Wall* for its documentary nature.

Hersey turned primarily to the writing of fiction in the late 1940s, but his greatest legacy may lie in the field of nonfiction, which he left permanently enriched. The enormous popularity of *Hiroshima* extended over the last half of the twentieth century. This guaranteed that Hersey's combination of dedication to precise fact and his strenuous and novelistic effort to sympathetically understand his subjects would remain a model for other nonfiction writers for decades.

## BIBLIOGRAPHY

Fishkin, Shelley Fisher. *From Fact to Fiction: Journalism and Imaginative Writing in America.* Baltimore: John Hopkins University Press, 1985.

Huse, Nancy Lyman. *John Hersey and James Agee: A Reference Guide.* Boston: G. K. Hall, 1978.

————. *The Survival Tales of John Hersey.* Troy, N.Y.: Whitston, 1983.

MacKinnon, Stephen R., and Oris Friesen. *China Reporting: An Oral History of American Journalism in the 1930s and 1940s.* Berkeley: University of California Press, 1987.

Sanders, David. *John Hersey Revisited.* Boston: Twayne Publishers, 1991.

Swanberg, W. A. *Luce and His Empire.* New York: Charles Scribner's Sons, 1972.

Walsh, Jeffrey. *American War Literature: 1914 to Vietnam.* New York: St. Martin's Press, 1982.

Weber, Ronald. *The Literature of Fact: Literary Nonfiction in American Writing.* Athens: Ohio University Press, 1980.

White, Theodore. *In Search of History: A Personal Narrative.* New York: Harper and Row, 1978.

Zavarzadeh, Mas'ud. *The Mythopoeic Reality: The Postwar American Nonfiction Novel.* Urbana: University of Illinois Press, 1976.

## LONG FICTION

| | |
|---|---|
| 1944 | A Bell for Adano |
| 1950 | The Wall |
| 1953 | The Marmot Drive |
| 1956 | A Single Pebble |
| 1959 | The War Lover |
| 1960 | The Child Buyer |
| 1965 | White Lotus |
| 1966 | Too Far to Walk |
| 1967 | Under the Eye of the Storm |
| 1972 | The Conspiracy |
| 1974 | My Petition for More Space |
| 1977 | The Walnut Door |
| 1985 | The Call |
| 1991 | Antonietta |

## NONFICTION

| | |
|---|---|
| 1942 | Men on Bataan |
| 1943 | Into the Valley: A Skirmish of the Marines |
| 1946 | Hiroshima |
| 1962 | Here to Stay: Studies in Human Tenacity |
| 1968 | The Algiers Motel Incident |
| 1970 | Letter to the Alumni |
| 1975 | The President |
| 1980 | Aspects of the Presidency: Truman and Ford in Office |
| 1985 | Hiroshima: A New Edition with a Final Chapter Written Forty Years after the Explosion |
| 1989 | Life Sketches |

## SHORT FICTION

| | |
|---|---|
| 1987 | Blues |
| 1990 | Fling and Other Stories |
| 1994 | Key West Tales |

## EDITED TEXTS

| | |
|---|---|
| 1974 | Ralph Ellison: A Collection of Critical Essays |
| 1974 | The Writer's Craft |

# Reader's Guide to Major Works

## A BELL FOR ADANO

**Genre:** Novel
**Subgenre:** Tragicomedy
**Published:** New York, 1944
**Time period:** 1943
**Setting:** Adano, Italy

**Themes and Issues.** The need for courage in the face of adversity, the strongest and most recurrent theme in Hersey's work, appears transformed in *A Bell for Adano*. In this novel the need for integrity in the face of resistance, temptation, and stupidity is embodied in Major Victor Joppolo, the central figure. "He was a good man, though weak in certain attractive, human ways," Hersey writes in the novel's foreword. While his being a "good man" does not prove to be enough for survival in the long run, his conduct is exemplary.

Joppolo's story is offered as a model for readers: "What he did and what he was not able to do in Adano represented in miniature what Americans can and cannot do in Europe," Hersey says. The novel's light tone and theatrical characters, who are largely colorful but essentially flat caricatures, reinforce the allegorical and instructive nature of the novel. Hersey's allegorical approach became more pronounced in such later novels as *The Marmot Drive*.

A still from the 1945 film version of *A Bell for Adano*, which starred John Hodiak as Major Joppolo. In Hersey's tale, the arrival of the bell offers a glimmer of hope that order would one day be restored.

**The Plot.** Major Joppolo is the Allied Military Government Occupied Territory's civil affairs officer for the small Italian town of Adano. When he inquires about the town's most pressing needs, he is given two answers: The townspeople need food, and they want their church's bell returned. The bell, a central feature of Adano's daily life, was taken away to be melted for wartime use just before the Allied invasion. Joppolo promises to do what he can. In the meantime he starts the process of getting the town back on its feet, dealing with difficulties in an even-handed and judicious manner.

Joppolo's biggest problem appears not from within Adano but from outside it, when an impatient General Marvin drives toward town and grows frustrated with slow-moving carts. He shoots a mule and commands Joppolo to prohibit carts from entering the town. Joppolo follows the general's orders, but then revokes them, knowing the town cannot survive otherwise.

Despite the high regard Joppolo wins from the townspeople and his love for his work, his disobedience results, in the end, in his dismissal and reassignment. Although his reassignment is a personal defeat, Joppolo is triumphant in his official role. Adano's people are content, particularly because Joppolo manages to obtain a U.S. Navy bell that is suitable for the town's church.

**Analysis.** *A Bell for Adano* was the first American novel to deal with the occupation of Italy, a circumstance made possible by Hersey's presence during the invasion and his swift composition of the novel immediately afterward. Appearing in magazine form in January 1944 and published in book form the next month, it posed the question of how the Allies might occupy conquered nations in an enlightened way, raising the issue long before most people were thinking beyond the ongoing war itself. Although Italy had surrendered in September 1943, the war would continue in Europe until May 1945. In the same month, *A Bell for Adano* was awarded the Pulitzer Prize for fiction.

The novel dramatized the general public sentiment that the United States, as a nation, could help to make the world a better place. Although it was criticized by some as overly simplified, the novel's buoyant spirit and easily grasped message continued to win new readers for decades. As a largely optimistic look at people's ability to control their own destinies, it stands in contrast to Hersey's subsequent novels, in which his optimism is tempered by an increasingly unsettled view of the world.

## SOURCES FOR FURTHER STUDY

Dee, Jonathan. "The Art of Fiction XCII: John Hersey." *Paris Review*, Summer/Fall 1986.

Hersey, John. "AMGOT at Work." *Life*, August 1943.

McDonnell, Thomas P. "Hersey's Allegorical Novels." *Catholic World*, July 1962.

Sanders, David. *John Hersey Revisited.* Boston: Twayne Publishers, 1991.

## HIROSHIMA

**Genre:** Nonfiction
**Subgenre:** Contemporary history
**Published:** New York, 1946
**Time period:** 1945
**Setting:** Hiroshima, Japan

**Themes and Issues.** In Hersey's great nonfiction novel, the courage that makes survival possible against great odds is not an attribute of the exceptional few, but rather a characteristic of those in every walk of life. Adversity can transform people into heroes, even if the heroism may seem small in comparison to the cause—in this case, the atom bomb.

A central motif of *Hiroshima* is that modern scientific technology is a threat to traditional values and institutions, an idea that reappears strikingly in *A Single Pebble*. Also central is the figure of the "good man." The victims of the bomb act in exemplary ways and are weak only in "human ways," as was *A Bell for Adano*'s Major Joppolo.

**The Plot.** Although the story in this nonfiction novel is not a plot in the traditional sense, it is indistinguishable from one in many respects.

The six central characters are Toshiko Sasaki, a clerk at a tin works; Dr. Masakazu Fujii, owner of a private hospital; Hatsuyo Nakamura, a tailor's widow; Father Wilhelm Kleinsorge, a Jesuit priest; Dr. Terufumi Sasaki of the city's Red Cross Hospital; and Kiyoshi Tanimoto, a Methodist pastor. Far from being anonymous mass victims of the dropping of the atom bomb, the six people face separate challenges to their survival, their talents, and their understanding. The characters are introduced at a point just before the moment of the bomb explosion, and the narrative follows them as they move into a world that is utterly transformed, and they encounter the greatest crisis of their lives.

At the time of the blast, Tanimoto was two miles distant, helping to move furniture. Mrs. Nakamura, only three-quarters of a mile from the epicenter, is buried within her house with her children. Dr. Fujii, only slightly farther from the epicenter, is thrown with his entire private hospital into the river, where he finds himself trapped among its beams. Father Kleinsorge, who had been feeling ill and was lying down in a room, went out of his mind briefly when the bomb hit and finds himself moments later walking outside, dazed and wounded. Dr. Sasaki chanced to be in a protected spot within the Red Cross Hospital and suddenly discovers that he is the lone doctor who is unhurt. Miss Sasaki, unrelated to Dr. Sasaki, is instantly buried beneath a collapsing ceiling and falling books, which break her leg.

Because of their relative good luck, Dr. Sasaki and the Rev. Tanimoto are soon kept busy helping others. Even this activity is not what it might have been in other circumstances, however. "Dr. Sasaki lost all sense of profession and stopped working as a skillful surgeon and a sympathetic man; he became an automaton, mechanically wiping, daubing, winding, wiping, daubing, winding." All six individuals fight for the preservation of their own and others' humanity. Rather than being en-

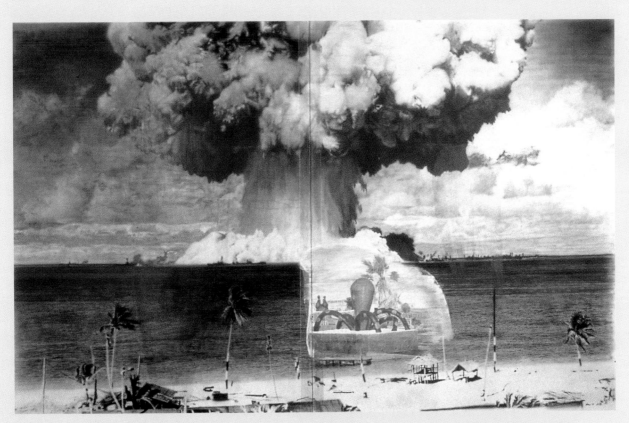

*Bikini*, a 1987 image by Vernon Fisher, references the power and destruction ushered in with the Atomic Age. Hersey's *Hiroshima* helped to personalize and humanize the disaster. The words of Miss Sasaki, Dr. Fujii, Mrs. Nakamura, Father Kleinsorge, Dr. Sasaki, and the Reverend Tanimoto gave a face to the otherwise countless casualties.

larged by their abilities to survive, however, they all emerge feeling diminished.

**Analysis.** To depict the horror of life after the atom bomb strike, Hersey describes events with meticulous attention to detail, carefully excluding any sensational material not directly pertaining to the story of the six survivors. This understatement helps to underline the everyday nature of the lives being disrupted, which in turn makes it feel grippingly real to readers, who can easily imagine their own everyday worlds similarly shattered.

The fictional approach, which enlarged the human lives under examination to dimensions larger than the political and military elements that gave rise to their difficulties, gives the book its sense of immediacy and universality.

## SOURCES FOR FURTHER STUDY

Guilfoil, Kelsey. "John Hersey: Fact and Fiction." *English Journal*, September 1950.

Sanders, David. "John Hersey: War Correspondent into Novelist." In *New Voices in American Studies*, edited by Ray B. Browne. Lafayette, Ind.: Purdue University Press, 1966.

Widmer, Kingsley. "American Apocalypse: Notes on the Bomb and the Failure of the Imagination." In *The Forties: Fiction, Poetry, and Drama*, edited by Warren B. French. Deland, Fla.: Everett/Edwards, 1969.

## THE WALL

**Genre:** Novel
**Subgenre:** Documentary history
**Published:** New York, 1950
**Time period:** 1939–1943
**Setting:** Warsaw, Poland

**Themes and Issues.** Hersey's first novel explored the potential of individuals to guarantee stability; his second, and perhaps most ambitious, novel develops a different theme. In *The Wall*, groups, not individuals, are of tanta-

German soldiers expel Polish Jews from their homes in the Warsaw ghetto in the period leading up to World War II. The image captures a facet of the intolerance and inhumanity Hersey wrote about in his 1950 novel *The Wall*.

mount importance. The unity created by pooling the talents of various individuals can be more important to the survival of an individual than the courage and integrity of that one individual alone.

In distinct counterpoint to this theme, Hersey introduces the character of observer and narrator Noach Levinson, an archivist who obsessively records everything possible. He writes down not only his own impressions but those of everyone around him, all of whom willingly share their experiences. As the narrative progresses, the once-isolated Levinson tentatively begins to accept the idea of belonging to a family, which consists of friends forced to live together in the ever more circumscribed Jewish ghetto in Warsaw. Eventually Levinson becomes a resistance fighter, as much as his physical limitations allow. The central fact of his importance, however, is that without his archive not even memories might survive.

Noach Levinson's heroism consists of his dedication to his mission. Nothing matters more to him than his records. Hersey reinforces this fact with the very structure of the novel. The story is presented as edited excerpts from Levinson's journals, which have survived the events described in their own pages. In this, as in other Hersey works, the lone individual triumphs against staggering odds through integrity and courage.

Just as Hersey used a foreword in *A Bell for Adano* to underline Major Joppolo's nature as a "good man," he wrote an editorial prologue to

Hersey's writing taps into the power of witness. Many of his works are culled from testimony, interviews, and first-hand accounts. Honoring the memory of the Japanese fishermen who died from the aftereffects of atomic testing, Ben Shahn's 1960 painting *The Lucky Dragon* draws similar inspiration from those who were there.

*The Wall* to establish the main character firmly. "One sunny day in the summer after the end of the war," it begins, "a search party found the Levinson Archive buried in seventeen iron boxes and a number of small parcels. . . ." By the time the main story begins, the reader already has a clear idea of who Levinson is and what his archive means, just as the reader has met Joppolo before the opening scene of *A Bell for Adano*.

**The Plot.** *The Wall* opens with the introduction of Dolek Berson, a man whom Levinson calls "a drifter: he lets life carry him along in its stream. . . ." Berson becomes an "Accidental Public Servant," a stand-in for a Jewish Community Council member who fails to appear when summoned by the Germans. Berson is imprisoned along with Levinson, who is a member.

After increasingly restricting the Jews in Warsaw and forcing them to build a wall around their ghetto, the Germans then "resettle" them, loading them onto trains for the death camp Treblinka. During these events, Levinson observes Berson gradually acquire purpose and direction. The archivist notes numerous individuals who acquire a deepening courage, especially Rachel Apt, a friend of both men.

Levinson also worries about divisions within the community: "Why is it that whenever men are in danger and have a clear-cut, dreadful adversary, they turn on each other in hatred?" Not until hundreds of thousands have been sent to Treblinka do the factions join into one coordinated resistance group. Both Berson and Apt become leading figures in the fight against the Germans, fleeing only when it becomes obvious that the ghetto is doomed.

**Analysis.** *The Wall*, a collection of diverse testimonies, is a novel in the form of documentary history. Fiction disguised as nonfiction, it anticipated *The Child Buyer*, which takes the form of a series of testimonies at a hearing. However, *The Wall* also echoes *Hiroshima* as a document based upon real lives and real incidents. Although *Hiroshima* was built on some thirty interviews conducted over a relatively brief span, *The Wall* was the result of two years of research on Hersey's part. Just as he relied on translators to speak with many survivors of the atom bomb, he used translators to give him access to original documents relating to the Warsaw ghetto, the death camps, and the uprising. Like *A Bell for Adano*, it was the first American novel on its subject.

## SOURCES FOR FURTHER STUDY

Geismar, Maxwell. *American Moderns: From Rebellion to Conformity*. New York: Hill & Wang, 1958.

Huse, Nancy Lyman. *The Survival Tales of John Hersey*. Troy, N.Y.: Whitston, 1983.

Langer, Lawrence L. *The Holocaust and the Literary Imagination*. New Haven, Conn.: Yale University Press, 1975.

# *Other Works*

**THE CHILD BUYER** (1960). John Hersey wrote *The Child Buyer* as both an exposé and a speculative exploration of a problem in American education. The novel has a strong satirical component, depicting politicians as simple minded and society as so worshipful of money that even the most high minded will betray their principles for the right price.

*The Child Buyer* takes the unusual form of a transcript of a hearing held by the State Senate Standing Committee on Education, Welfare, and Public Morality, in an unnamed state. The senators are considering a baffling situation: "It is alleged that on October sixteenth . . . a certain Mr. Wissey Jones entered the town of Pequot from out of State, and that he did conspire with persons in the town in an attempt to purchase a male white child, ten years of age, named Barry Rudd, advancing unspecified educational and patriotic purposes for the proposed transaction."

Senate members Mansfield, Skypack, and Voyoko interview teachers, school administrators, Rudd's parents, and the brilliant child himself. They also interview Jones, representative of United Lymphomilloid, a corporation in need of brilliant children.

Jones testifies as to the inability of America's educational system to identify and assist the most talented of its children. After various community members voice their initial reservations and objections, Jones soothes them with substantial bribes, with the result that their final testimonies swing in United Lymphomilloid's favor.

Jones then unveils his reasons for needing the child: A scientific project will use Barry Rudd's mind as it has never been used before, as part of a biological computer—but only after obliterating Barry's existing personality. The child, unswayed by bribery, gives his own consent to the project in the end—not out of desire that his mind be used to its full potential, but in order to prove that he can survive, as a separate personality, even against the threat of complete erasure of everything he knows.

## INTO THE VALLEY: A SKIRMISH OF THE MARINES
(1943). On the surface, Hersey's second book, *Into the Valley*, is much like his first, *Men on Bataan*: a patriotic report on the war, intended to inform and uplift. Yet a new sensibility pervades *Into the Valley*. "On the eighth day of October in the first year of our war," Hersey writes, "I went down into a valley with Captain Charles Rigaud of the United States Marines. A small skirmish took place down there."

The story that follows is simple in its outline. Rigaud leads his Marines into a valley as part of a coordinated attempt to wrest it from occupying Japanese troops. They walk into an ambush. Under fire, Hersey observes the fear in the troops and in himself, and the courage displayed by Rigaud.

While the skirmish was only part of an action called the Third Battle of the Matanikau River, which was in turn part of a larger action on Guadalcanal Island, Hersey avoids describing the larger picture and focuses on individual events and characters, much as a novelist would. His close focus, moreover, has the effect of enlarging his observations. "The valley was on Guadalcanal Island, but it might have been anywhere," he says.

As with many Hersey books—nonfiction and fiction alike—*Into the Valley* carries a moral burden. Hersey hoped that as a realistic portrayal of the feelings of the Marines at war it would help reading audiences to understand the experience of battle, and in so doing, help ensure future peace.

Marines huddle in a part of Guadalcanal Island known as "Hell's Corner." Japanese troops, retreating along the river, skirmished with a small group of Marines there in 1942. Hersey spent several weeks in the fall of 1942 on Guadalcanal Island, where he accompanied U.S. Marines into battle.

**A SINGLE PEBBLE** (1956). Hersey's fourth novel represented a departure for the now well-established author. Hersey was already known for his novels of contemporary history, and in *A Single Pebble* he looked to 1920s China in this drama pitting Western arrogance against Eastern tradition.

A young Western engineer travels upstream on the Yangtze River in a Chinese-manned junk. The engineer represents a contracting firm hoping to sell the Chinese government on a power-generating dam on the mighty river. He is convinced of Western superiority but nevertheless finds himself fascinated by a powerful man named Old Pebble, who from the shore leads the crew that pulls the boat by ropes upstream against the current. He also finds himself falling in love with the boat owner's wife, who tends to him when he falls ill.

With the Yangtze's waters rising, and with passage upstream growing more hazardous by the day, the engineer begins to see Old Pebble's heroic labors as part of a long-formalized tradition stretching back thousands of years. He gains a more compassionate understanding, but not until after he has fatally disrupted Old Pebble's inner balance.

# Resources

John Hersey's manuscripts are held in the John Hersey Special Collection at Yale University's Beinecke Rare Book and Manuscript Library. Manuscripts of correspondence can also be found elsewhere in the university's holdings, including the Beinecke Library's Robert Penn Warren and Sinclair Lewis collections. Other sources of interest to students of Hersey include the following:

**John Hersey High School.** Opened in 1968, with its first class graduating in 1970, the John Hersey High School serves the communities of Arlington Heights, Prospect Heights, and Mount Prospect, Illinois. Hersey supported the school, making several visits and sending minor contributions to its publications. (http://jhhs.dist214.k12.il.us/)

**The Nuclear Files.** A Web site sponsored by the Nuclear Age Peace Foundation features a comprehensive bibliography called the "Enola Gay Exhibit Controversy Readings," prepared by the Historian's Committee for Open Debate on Hiroshima. The bibliography references books, journals, and magazine articles that deal with the Hiroshima issue. (http://www.nuclearfiles.org/bibl/enola-gay.html).

**"The Publication of 'Hiroshima' in *The New Yorker*."** An essay written by Steve Rothman and available on line discusses the writing, editing, and unusual publication history of Hersey's book. (http://www.geocities.com/Heartland/Hills/6556/hiro.html).

**The Herseys in America.** This genealogical Web site gives insight into the family of John Hersey and its history in the United States. (http://gwis2.circ.gwo.edu/~shersey/america.htm).

**Audio Recordings.** The Audio Partners Publishing Corporation offers an audio version of *Hiroshima*, read by Edward Asner and produced in 1995. Books on Tape also offers a 1981 audio version of the book, read by Dan Lazar. Other Books on Tape titles by Hersey include *A Bell for Adano* (1981), *The Child Buyer* (1981), *The Conspiracy* (1980), and *The War Lover* (1978), all read by Lazar. A John Hersey interview with Kay Bonetti (1988) is available from the American Audio Prose Library.

*MARK RICH*

# S. E. Hinton

**BORN:** July 22, 1948, Tulsa, Oklahoma
**IDENTIFICATION:** Late-twentieth-century writer of young-adult novels and children's stories, four of which have been made into films.

S. E. Hinton changed the tone and substance of young-adult fiction with her first published novel, *The Outsiders* (1967). Dissatisfied with the portrayals of teenagers in traditional adolescent novels, she wrote her popular story of class conflict and gang rivalry while in high school. Readers and critics appreciated her narrative style and her skill in creating a swiftly moving plot and convincing characters. Unlike previous teenage novels, Hinton's novels, such as *The Outsiders*, *That Was Then, This Is Now* (1971), and *Rumble Fish* (1975), feature idealistic teenagers who cope with such real challenges as parental absence or neglect, violence, poverty, class prejudice, alcoholism, and drug addiction, as well as love, hate, and loss.

Susan Eloise Hinton was born on July 22, 1948, in Tulsa, Oklahoma, to Mr. and Mrs. Grady P. Hinton. In 1963 she became a student at Tulsa's Will Rogers High School, which would become the model for the setting of *The Outsiders*. In her junior year (1964–1965) her father died of a cancerous brain tumor; during his illness, Hinton increasingly withdrew into herself and found solace in writing *The Outsiders*, the third novel she had written but the first to be published.

As a child Hinton enjoyed reading, a love that continued into her adolescence and included a number of the classics of English and American literature. However, she discovered little of interest in the books written for her age group and thought that she was not yet ready for most adult literature. She is often quoted as saying, "I wrote *The Outsiders* so I'd have something to read." One story has it that she earned a D in her junior English class while she was writing the novel; another story says that she learned while sitting on the stand at her high school graduation that it would be published.

**College Years.** *The Outsiders* sold over four million copies and enabled Hinton to attend the University of Tulsa, where she met her future husband, David Inhofe. There she wrote an essay, "Teen-Agers Are for Real," which was published in the *New York Times Book Review* in

Hinton (right) and actor Matt Dillon on the set of *Tex*, the 1982 motion-picture adaptation of Hinton's book by the same title. Hinton worked closely with director and cast, even playing a small role herself. Dillon, a major teenage heartthrob at the time, would later star in the film versions of two other Hinton novels, *The Outsiders* and *Rumble Fish*.

August 1967. She graduated in 1970 with a bachelor's degree in education. After overcoming a three-year writer's block with the encouragement of her husband, who assigned her to write two pages every day, she published *That Was Then, This Is Now* in 1971. She wrote two more novels in the 1970s, *Rumble Fish* and *Tex* (1979), and published *Taming the Star Runner* in 1988.

Hinton set out to write about the difficult social system that teenagers create among themselves. Her books struck a chord with readers who saw in her characters many elements of this system that existed in their own schools and towns. Her stories of confrontations between rival groups of teenagers were immediately successful with critics and young readers and won several awards. There was some controversy about the level of violence in her novels and in her other works, but Hinton's work was praised for its realistic dialogue.

During the 1980s Hinton collaborated on and supervised the production of four film adaptations of her books, including the commercially successful 1983 Francis Ford Coppola film based on *The Outsiders*. She also devoted time to her personal life in the 1980s, giving birth to a son, Nicholas David, in 1983. In 1995 she produced the first of two works for young children, *Big David, Little David*, which was followed by *The Puppy Sister* (1995).

**Hinton and Hollywood.** Four of Hinton's young-adult novels have appeared as films.

The 1983 film adaptation of Hinton's novel *The Outsiders* starred some of the biggest teenage actors of the day, some of them members of the notorious "Brat Pack," a verbal parody on singer Frank Sinatra's "Rat Pack." The all-star cast included (from left to right) Emilio Estevez, Rob Lowe, C. Thomas Howell, Matt Dillon, Ralph Macchio, Patrick Swayze, and Tom Cruise.

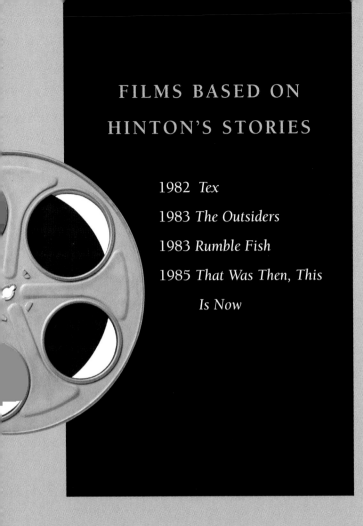

## FILMS BASED ON HINTON'S STORIES

1982  *Tex*

1983 *The Outsiders*

1983 *Rumble Fish*

1985 *That Was Then, This*

*Is Now*

Hinton did not rush to accept the production offers of the Disney company, however, fearing that the company would film something, she said, "like 'Tex and the Seven Dwarfs.'" However, critics agree that Hollywood has been generally faithful to her conceptions of story and characters. Tim Hunter directed *Tex*—the first of Hinton's stories to be filmed, released in September 1982—making certain that the film was true to the book. The film starred Matt Dillon as Tex McCormick, Jim Metzler as Mason McCormick, Meg Tilly as Jamie Collins, and Emilio Estevez as Johnny Collins.

Hunter shot the film on locations in and around Tulsa, Oklahoma, enlisting Hinton's help in selecting many of the locations, indicating something of the close working relationship that developed between Hunter and Hinton. Hinton also worked closely with the film's star, Matt Dillon. She even taught Dillon how to ride her horse, Toyota, who appears in the film as Tex's horse, Negrito. Hunter also persuaded Hinton herself to appear as Mrs.

Barnes, the typing teacher harassed by Tex's typewriter prank. *Tex* was well received by critics, who generally accounted the film to have been well acted and directed. It is Hinton's favorite of the four films.

The next of Hinton's novels to be filmed was *The Outsiders*. Directed by Francis Ford Coppola, it again starred Matt Dillon, as Dallas Winston. Other parts were played by such well-known actors as Patrick Swayze, Rob Lowe, Emilio Estevez, and Tom Cruise. The film opened in March 1983 and grossed over five million dollars in the first weekend of its release. *The Outsiders* was not considered the best of the Hinton screen adaptations; Kathleen Knutsen Rowell's screenplay was rewritten by several other writers, including Coppola, with some help from Hinton. Hinton was a paid consultant for the film and enjoyed her involvement, which included another cameo appearance as a nurse caring for Dallas.

Adapted next was *Rumble Fish*, with another starring role for Matt Dillon, as Rusty-James, and appearances by Dennis Hopper as Father, Mickey Rourke as Motorcycle Boy, Nicolas Cage as Smokey, and Tom Waits as Benny. Coppola directed this film and collaborated with Hinton on the screenplay, working on it on Sundays during the filming of *The Outsiders*. The film opened in October of 1983. Reviews were mixed: Some praised the film's use of eerie, allusive, mythical elements; others saw it as "overblown, operatic, pretentious." Shot in black and white to suggest Motorcycle Boy's color blindness, the film represents well the dark mood of the story. Only the fish are in color, red and blue, swimming around the black and white screen as if to suggest a fable without the constraints of space and time.

The last of Hinton's books to be filmed was *That Was Then, This Is Now*, directed by Christopher Cain and released by Paramount Pictures in November 1985. Hinton was not involved in the production, which starred several enduring actors, such as Emilio Estevez, Kim Delaney, and Morgan Freeman. Estevez

# HIGHLIGHTS IN HINTON'S LIFE

**1948**      Susan Eloise Hinton is born on July 22 in Tulsa, Oklahoma.

**1963**      Enters Tulsa's Will Rogers High School, the model for *The Outsiders*.

**1964–1965**      Writes *The Outsiders* during her father's terminal illness.

**1966**      Enrolls at the University of Tulsa.

**1967**      Publishes *The Outsiders*.

**1970**      Graduates from the University of Tulsa with a bachelor's degree in education; marries David Inhofe.

**1971**      Publishes *That Was Then, This Is Now*.

**1975**      Publishes *Rumble Fish*.

**1979**      Publishes *Tex*.

**1982**      Film version of *Tex* is released.

**1983**      Film version of *The Outsiders* is released; son, Nicholas David, is born; film version of *Rumble Fish* is released.

**1985**      Film version of *That Was Then, This Is Now* is released.

**1988**      Receives YASD/SLJ Author Achievement Award from the American Library Association; publishes *Taming the Star Runner*.

**1995**      Publishes two books for children, *Big David, Little David* and *The Puppy Sister*.

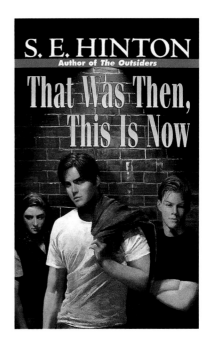

also wrote the screenplay, but the result was a less courageous and more conventional film than *Rumble Fish*.

In July of 1988 Hinton became the first recipient of the YASD/SLJ Author Achievement Award, given by the Young Adult Services Division of the American Library Association and the *School Library Journal* to an author whose "book or books, over a period of time, have been accepted by young adults as an authentic voice . . . [in] their lives." That same year, she published her fifth young-adult novel, *Taming the Star Runner*. In 1995 she published two books for children, *Big David, Little David* and *The Puppy Sister*.

S. E. Hinton wrote young-adult fiction, screenplays based on her novels, and children's stories. The most striking qualities of her five young-adult novels are their direct, clear style and their focus on boys in their early to middle teens. These young men are outsiders, often without parents, who find substitutes for their absent families by bonding with groups of other boys. Hinton's tone is consistently sympathetic to these troubled youths, who find their way despite the challenges of violence, abandonment, drugs, and poverty.

**Issues in Hinton's Fiction.** Hinton's constant aim has been to provide "realistic" fiction addressing the issues that faced her friends in high school instead of the prevailing themes of young-adult fiction of the 1940s and 1950s, with settings such as dances and football games. When Hinton was a junior in high school, her father died of brain cancer after a lengthy illness and hospitalization. This experience contributed to her withdrawal and her focus on issues of isolation, death, and the consequences of a father's disappearance from a teenager's life.

**People in Hinton's Fiction.** Hinton's novels feature young male characters who face serious challenges, such as parental abuse, neglect, or total abandonment. Their search for a father or an adequate substitute is met by a group of friends or a gang—other boys of similar age, background, and social and economic status. They face physical and psychological attacks from other gangs and from authorities, who are often insensitive to their situations. They engage in violence, use drugs, face racial and class prejudice, and sometimes find solace and purpose in their attachments to horses and rural environments.

**Themes in Hinton's Fiction.** In each of Hinton's novels, the parents are dead or they have disappeared because of divorce or abandonment. The result is that the boys make their own decisions and choices, always with serious consequences but often emerging from the experience with survivors' strength.

The theme of violence pervades Hinton's work. In her stories the world is a dangerous

Leslie Patterson's mixed-media artwork *Lost Button Owner Identification Calendar* reflects the search for a lost part of one's self. Like Patterson's subjects, characters in Hinton's fiction are missing something, usually the guidance of a father figure. The death of Hinton's own father while she was in high school is a contributing factor to this strong theme in her work.

# SOME INSPIRATIONS BEHIND HINTON'S WORK

S. E. Hinton grew up in Tulsa, Oklahoma, a former oil boomtown with a history of racial prejudice and ethnic-based violence. Opportunities for sudden wealth and grinding poverty were present in equal measure. Race-based tensions between whites and blacks, between whites and Native Americans directly, and between whites and Mexican Americans simmered below the surface and were part of the cultural context of much of Oklahoma.

The death of Hinton's father when she was sixteen contributed to the strong theme of loss in her work. In the dedication appearing at the end of the film *The Outsiders*, Hinton pays tribute to Jo Ellen Misakian, a librarian, and a group of seventh and eighth graders, students of the Lone Star School in Fresno, California, who first suggested that this book be made into a film.

Several pervasive myths allege direct autobiographical inspirations for Hinton's work. The most compelling of these origin stories says that Hinton witnessed a rumble, or gang fight, in which a young boy was killed and that she went home to write it out of her system.

However, the most significant influences on Hinton the writer are clearly her early reading and her family's dedication to hard and consistent work as the key to success. From her reading she absorbed a fundamental principle of American storytelling: to place characters into extreme situations and see what individual acts of valor or cowardice they will perform. *The Outsiders* was her first published novel, but she wrote two earlier, unpublished novels that taught her much about the craft of writing.

Hinton has repeatedly said that the lack of quality young-adult fiction available for her to read inspired her to write *The Outsiders*. The allusions to Charles Dickens's *Great Expectations* (1860–1861) and Ponyboy Curtis's recitation of Robert Frost's poem "Nothing Gold Can Stay" suggest that classical English and American literature are the most powerful influences on Hinton's work.

However, Hinton's experiences with the publisher who accepted *The Outsiders* as she was graduating from high school seem clearly to be the source for Travis's reactions and mistakes in *Taming the Star Runner* when he learns that his novel will be published. Travis begins the hard work of accepting his maturity and making productive use of the loss of his innocence, comfort, and friends. "He sat there, waiting" after rolling a blank sheet of paper into the typewriter to begin his second novel, much like S. E. Hinton, who took four years to write her second novel.

*Miranda in Springtime*, a 1998 oil painting by Kathryn Jacobi, echoes the peace and solitude of the inner self. Hinton's inner self became a safe haven from the outside world during her father's illness. Her writing and her love of horses brought her great comfort.

place in which the violent actions of contrasting forces test the boys' mettle. Consequences range from rejection to death, from acceptance to triumph, usually as the result of self-sacrifice. For example, Johnny kills Bob in a fight to save Ponyboy and later dies as result of an injury suffered while rescuing kids from a burning church.

The themes of time and change, free will and fate, and discipline and growth are tightly connected to each other in both *That Was Then, This Is Now* and *Taming the Star Runner*. Hinton suggests that one must change with time and exercise agency through discipline and growth to make the best of one's fate. Her work shows these themes as being pervasive from adolescence through adulthood.

Another common theme in Hinton's work is that of brothers and orphans. The state of being a brother or an orphan is as often a state of mind as one of literal circumstance. Blood ties are sometimes stronger than those of friendship, sometimes not. Most important is taking responsibility not only for one's own actions but also for the preservation and well-being of the other.

Always present in Hinton's novels are the themes of knowledge and the sacrifice of self. Her characters must learn their place in the world, and the forces that oppose them often strengthen the characters of those who survive, most notably Ponyboy Curtis and Travis. Sometimes, however, knowledge reduces a character to existential despair, as it does with Motorcycle Boy, whose discovery and accep-

tance of his mother's disappearance drives him to free the Rumble Fish, symbolic of his self-sacrifice that frees his peers from destructive gang fights.

## BIBLIOGRAPHY

Campbell, Patty. Review of *Taming the Star Runner*, by S. E. Hinton. *New York Times Book Review*, April 2, 1989, 26.

Daly, Jay. *Presenting S. E. Hinton*. Boston: Twayne Publishers, 1989.

Donelson, Kenneth L., and Alleen Pace Nilsen. *Literature for Today's Young Adults*. 3d ed. Glenview, Ill.: Scott, Foresman, 1989.

Hinton, S. E. "Advice from a Penwoman: An Interview with S. E. Hinton." Interview by Lisa Ehrichs. *Seventeen* 40 (November 1981): 32.

Malone, Michael. "Tough Puppies." *The Nation* 242, no. 9 (March 8, 1986): 276–278, 290.

Simmons, John S. "A Look Inside a Landmark: *The Outsiders*." In *Censored Books: Critical Viewpoints*, edited by John M. Kean. Metuchen, N.J.: Scarecrow, 1993.

Solomon, Charles. Review of *The Outsiders*, by S. E. Hinton. *Los Angeles Times Book Review*, August 12, 1990, 10.

Stanek, Lou Willett. *A Teacher's Guide to the Paperback Editions of the Novels of S. E. Hinton*. 1975. Rev. ed. New York: Dell, 1980.

Sutherland, Zena. "The Teen-Ager Speaks." *Saturday Review of Literature*, November 19, 1968, 34.

VanderStaay, Steven L. "Doing Theory: Words About Words About *The Outsiders*." *English Journal* 81, no.7 (November 1992): 57–61.

## LONG FICTION

1967  The Outsiders
1971  That Was Then, This Is Now
1975  Rumble Fish
1979  Tex
1988  Taming the Star Runner

## CHILDREN'S LITERATURE

1995  Big David, Little David
1995  The Puppy Sister

# *Hinton's Characters*

S. E. Hinton has claimed that her books all show character growth in some way. The changes that take place in the major figures of her young-adult novels suggest that she has been largely successful in this aim, although there are exceptions. From the beginning of her career Hinton was crowned Queen of the New Realism, and her works dominated young-adult fiction.

Hinton's novels, the argument goes, present a realistic view of the teenage world of the 1960's and 1970's because they present teens who face contemporary and gritty challenges that force them to change in order to overcome them. However, critic Michael Malone offered a powerful counterargument in a 1986 essay in *The Nation*, arguing that Hinton's novels are neither representative of average American teenagers nor as realistic as they have been alleged to be. Malone asserts that the appeal of Hinton's works among teenage readers lies mainly in their action-packed narratives, simplistic plot structures, intense emotional tone, and well-defined principles.

**Sympathetic Identification.** Young-adult readers and their teachers certainly recognize the changes that Hinton's "lost boys" go through. Even if readers do not recognize the specific challenges that Hinton's characters face, they can respond to the intensity of feelings expressed in her fiction. However, challenge and change do not necessarily mean growth. If growth results from characters' doing battle with those biological and sociological "givens" of the fiction, then their growth is a matter of a self-awareness that is more recognizable on mythic and psychological levels than on the "realistic" surfaces of street life.

Matt Dillon in the role of Rusty-James exudes the perfect combination of toughness and anger that are pervasive qualities in many of Hinton's characters. He is flanked from left to right by fellow *Rumble Fish* cast members Nicholas Cage, Vincent Spano, and Christopher Penn.

**Revelation and Growth.** Character growth results from the "fall from innocence into experience," such as the archetypal Garden of Eden story of Eve's eating the apple. Such an archetype is best compressed into a short and intense period of days, weeks, or months at most. Hinton's genius lies in her crafting this intense period of revelation and growth of understanding into, as Malone asserts, action-packed narratives of situations that produce traumatic experiences of physical and psychological pain.

The experiences are archetypal in that they often involve uncertainty about one's identity (including knowledge of one's parents), parental abandonment, violence suffered at the hands of fathers and rivals, conflicts with authority figures, the development of romantic relationships, and the loss of formerly meaningful relationships. In all of these areas, the struggle provides instruction and opportunities for growth and forces the young men to come to terms with their experiences and their new knowledge. Some emerge triumphant with the gift of life, with which they will return to their "village" to reinvigorate its life; some are destroyed, defeated by overwhelming forces, which include their own fundamental character flaws of disaffection, ennui, and rage.

Violence is a common thread in Hinton's novels. Her characters often experience great physical and psychological pain. Here, in one of the many rumbles that take place in Hinton's stories, actor Matt Dillon (right) spars with actor Glenn Withrow in a typical dark scene from the movie *Rumble Fish*.

The characters Tex and Mason, played by actors Matt Dillon (left) and Jim Metzler in the 1982 film adaptation of Hinton's novel *Tex*, possess characteristics that help them not only to survive but to succeed. Not all Hinton characters are able to muster the strength or grit that make the transition possible.

**Importance of Setting.** Another element to consider is the contrast between the pastoral and urban worlds that are the stages for Hinton's fictions. All her novels move back and forth from urban to rural settings and back again, from the relative security and purposefulness of pastoral life to the savagery and darkness of the city, whether in alleys, pool halls, and gang rumbles or in the garish falseness of the sideshows and fortune-tellers and thrill rides at the fair. All Hinton's characters have been expelled from Eden. All are looking for messages from their "fathers" to guide them through life.

**Those Who Stay.** Those of Hinton's characters who survive their experiences arrive—battered and wounded, perhaps—with a degree of self-knowledge. They earn a better understanding of their existential situations, of the obstacles that face them, and of the opportunities that await them.

Because the goal of each of the orphans is to mitigate his lack of a family by finding an appropriate substitute family, the way that each accommodates to the realities of his quest and its results suggests growth. Those such as Travis and Tex, the central figures of Hinton's last two novels, achieve a promising measure of success through their acceptance by adults into the world of work and responsibility. At the end of *Taming the Star Runner,* Travis rolls a sheet of paper into his typewriter to begin his second novel; at the end of *Tex,* Tex has a job at Kincaide's stables, reconciles with his older half-brother Mason, and accepts that he will be one of "those who stay." However, characters such as Dallas Winston, Motorcycle Boy, and Johnny Cade seem fated by a bad combination of nature and nurture to fail in their quests. It seems these young men have a destiny from which they cannot escape.

Hinton's most successful characters discover and create ways of accommodating their fates and moving forward. Their experiences change their views of the world. Their potential takes them far, perhaps even so far as to create their own successful families and thus to compensate for the loss of their birth families. In these ways some—though not all—of Hinton's characters grow toward productivity and responsible membership in the adult community: Uncle Ken respects the capable and increasingly responsible Travis. Mr. Kincaide and Cole Collins accept and respect Tex McCormick.

## SOURCES FOR FURTHER STUDY

Daly, Jay. *Presenting S. E. Hinton.* Boston: Twayne Publishers, 1989.

Malone, Michael. "Tough Puppies." *The Nation* 242, no. 9 (March 8, 1986): 276–278, 290.

Mills, Randall K. "The Novels of S. E. Hinton: Springboard to Personal Growth for Adolescents." *Adolescence* 22 (Fall 1987): 641–646.

# Reader's Guide to Major Works

## THE OUTSIDERS

**Genre:** Novel
**Subgenre:** Young-adult fiction
**Published:** New York, 1967
**Time period:** 1960s
**Setting:** Tulsa, Oklahoma

**Themes and Issues.** S. E. Hinton's first novel established several themes that figure prominently in all of her young-adult fiction: adolescent males, often brothers, who must fend for themselves without parents and without economic security; social and class distinctions that become the basis for gang fights; violence that sometimes leads to death and that is fatalistically accepted; and antagonism that exists between the heroes and various authority figures, who include police, teachers, and other adults. Courage, perseverance, and education as a means of survival are also important themes.

**The Plot.** The "outsiders" in this novel are the greasers—Ponyboy, Sodapop, Darrel ("Darry") Curtis, and others in their gang: Steve Randle, Two-Bit Matthews, Dallas ("Dally") Winston, and Johnny Cade. Ponyboy and Johnny are attacked by some members of a rival gang, the Socs, one night after Ponyboy and Johnny talk to "their" girls at a drive-in movie. Johnny, who has previously been seriously beaten by a Soc, kills Bob after the Socs nearly drown Ponyboy. Ponyboy and Johnny hop a freight train out of town. They hide out at an abandoned church that Dally knows about. The church catches fire, and Johnny and Ponyboy become heroes by rescuing a group of children who have stumbled into the church, but Johnny is injured and dies later in the hospital.

**Analysis.** *The Outsiders* is recognized as the beginning of realistic young-adult fiction and has been wildly popular in school classrooms, perhaps because its characters cope with violence, poverty, alcoholism, and drug addiction. Hinton presents her themes in a straightforward style, in a skillfully developed plot, and with characters with whom teen readers of the 1970s and 1980s identified. It was one of

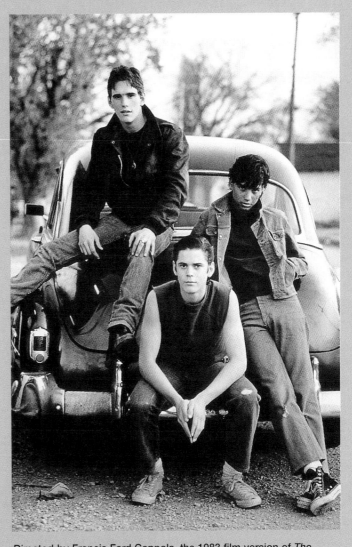

Directed by Francis Ford Coppola, the 1983 film version of *The Outsiders* was the most successful of the four motion pictures adapted from Hinton's books, grossing over five million dollars in its opening weekend. Actors Matt Dillon (left) played Dallas, C. Thomas Howell (center) played Ponyboy, and Ralph Macchio (right) played Johnny.

the first young-adult novels that dealt with adolescent social groups in ways teenagers actually viewed them. Despite, or perhaps because of, its gritty and often violent realism, the novel's message of friendship, sympathy, and understanding remains fresh and appealing.

## SOURCES FOR FURTHER STUDY

Daly, Jay. "*The Outsiders*: Staying Gold." In *Presenting S. E. Hinton*. Boston: Twayne Publishers, 1989.

Pearlman, Michael. "The Role of Socioeconomic Status in Adolescent Literature." *Adolescence* 30 (Spring 1995): 223–231.

Simmons, John S. "A Look Inside a Landmark: *The Outsiders*." In *Censored Books: Critical Viewpoints*, edited by John M. Kean. Metuchen, N.J.: Scarecrow, 1993.

TEX
**Genre:** Novel
**Subgenre:** Young-adult fiction
**Published:** New York, 1979
**Time period:** Late 1960s
**Setting:** Bixby, Oklahoma

**Themes and Issues.** Tex and Mason have been abandoned for all practical purposes by Pop. This leaves them to deal with poverty, drugs, violence, illegitimacy, brotherhood, the loss of innocence, friendship, and coming-of-age.

**The Plot.** Texas McCormick, age fifteen, and his seventeen-year-old brother, Mason, live on their own in a run-down house. Their mother is dead, and their father is an ex-convict who is away for months at a time on the rodeo circuit. The

Hinton's novels, particularly *Tex*, explore a loss of innocence and the relationship between brothers. Bo Bartlett's 1993 oil painting *Firefly*, depicting that brief period at dusk when fireflies light up, captures the fleeting nature of childhood as the sun sets on another day.

McCormicks live near the well-to-do Collins family, and Tex is best friends with Johnny Collins. Johnny's father, Cole Collins, is afraid that Tex and Mason will corrupt his children. Mason, a basketball star at the high school, is determined to finish school and go to college.

When Mason sells the family's horses, including Tex's Negrito, to pay the bills, Tex is brokenhearted and angry at Mason, and reconciliation is difficult. Mason's friend Lem is a drug dealer, and Tex is nearly killed in a delivery gone wrong. Tex calls his "girlfriend," Jamie Collins, whose father, Cole, sends an ambulance. Tex also learns that Pop is not his biological father and comes to accept that he will never get Negrito back.

**Analysis.** *Tex* continues Hinton's exploration of the challenges facing teenage boys who grow up in the absence of a stable home life and who must deal on their own with issues of sex, violence, economic disparities, drugs, and the usual problems of adolescence and school life. Tex and Mason especially face parental indifference and absence. Tex is innocent but also tough-minded and solidly honest; by the end of the novel he becomes more clearly aware of the existence of evil.

## SOURCES FOR FURTHER STUDY

Daly, Jay. "*Tex*: Those Who Go and Those Who Stay." In *Presenting S. E. Hinton*. Boston: Twayne Publishers, 1989.

Mills, Randall K. "The Novels of S. E. Hinton: Springboard to Personal Growth for Adolescents." *Adolescence* 22 (Fall 1987): 641–646.

Stanek, Lou Willett. *A Teacher's Guide to the Paperback Editions of the Novels of S. E. Hinton*. 1975. Rev. ed. New York: Dell, 1980.

## TAMING THE STAR RUNNER

    **Genre:** Novel
    **Subgenre:** Young-adult fiction
    **Published:** New York, 1988
    **Time period:** 1960s
    **Setting:** Tulsa, Oklahoma

**Themes and Issues.** Hinton's fifth young-adult novel adds the theme of creativity to her established format of an adolescent boy rebelling against authority, seeking friendship and acceptance, and discovering the consequences of his actions while making his own way without useful parental guidance. Travis Harris is a young writer, a creator of worlds of words and emotions. Thus, he is the first of Hinton's central figures to face his future with a solidly positive, if unconventional, focus. Ironically, perhaps, Hinton seems to have a greater aesthetic distance from Travis than she does from the central characters of her earlier books. Finally, the horse Star Runner—wild, powerful, talented, dangerous, and untamed— surely suggests the nature of the creative force, which must be trained and disciplined to achieve its full potential. Otherwise, it collides with other forces of nature and is destroyed.

**The Plot.** Sixteen-year-old Travis Harris's stepfather, Stan, burns Travis's stories and poems. Travis becomes enraged and nearly kills Stan with a poker. Travis is then sent to his uncle Ken's horse ranch near Cleveland, Oklahoma. There he finds himself in a new and different world—rural, small-town, and very slow, compared with the fast life he had been used to in Los Angeles.

Travis has a secret. Although he is a hood who likes to smoke, drink, and speed dangerously on the California freeways, he is also a writer. He teaches himself to type in the sixth grade so that he can type ninety words a minute by the time he actually takes typing class in school. In the process he writes stories. Exiled on the horse ranch, Travis goes to school with "hick jocks and hick nerds" who do not realize how cool he is. His attitude wins him no friends; consequently, he is mostly ignored by his new classmates.

Out of loneliness, he begins to hang around his uncle's horse barn, where eighteen-year-old Casey Kencaide has a riding school. Travis watches Casey work with her gray stallion, Star Runner, and finds himself falling in love with her. Casey hires him to muck out stalls, help with the tack, and rub down the horses. Travis then gets a letter from a publisher accepting a

David Levinthal's untitled 1988 image reflects the wild beauty of Star Runner and the taming of the dangerous force in Travis, the main character in Hinton's *Taming the Star Runner*. Hinton herself longed to be a cowboy and have a horse when she was growing up, an idea that seemed strange to her at the time but seems perfectly natural to her as an adult.

novel that he has written. After meeting with the publisher, who flies to Tulsa to see him, he is ecstatic but has trouble finding someone to share his pleasure. When Casey wins a difficult jumping competition with Star Runner at a horse show, Travis kisses her and grudgingly admits what he had felt was the "strange tie, bond, fate, between them."

Travis's old friend Joe shows up in Oklahoma, having fled Los Angeles. Joe has been terrified by the double murder of Billie and Mike—twin friends of Travis and Joe—by the malevolent Orson. Orson manages a record store where drug users congregate, but he also runs a gang of thieves. Travis and Casey pick Joe up and install him in Travis's room. Uncle Ken advises Joe and helps him return to testify against Orson. Travis realizes that he may have escaped from his old life just in time.

As if the emotional tumult were not enough, a tornado strikes. Star Runner leaps the fence and gallops off across the fields, with Casey

A lack of parental guidance is the classic trademark of Hinton's fiction. Parents are either nonexistent or have, for whatever reason, turned their back on their children's needs. Duncan Hannah's 1989 oil painting *Betrayal* evokes the banishment of Travis from his stepfather's home in Hinton's 1988 novel, *Taming the Star Runner*.

and Travis in wild, exultant pursuit in a Jeep. Lightning strikes, knocking Travis and Casey unconscious. They awake to an empty pasture and a smell of burning flesh, suggesting that Star Runner has been killed. Travis's passion for Casey has been replaced by a close friendship, and he settles in, as the book ends, to begin a second novel.

**Analysis.** In July of 1988 Hinton became the first recipient of the YASD/SLJ Author Achievement Award, given by the Young Adult Services Division of the American Library Association and the *School Library Journal* to an author whose "book or books, over a period of time, have been accepted by young adults as an authentic voice . . . [in] their lives."

In October of the same year she published *Taming the Star Runner*, clearly her most assured and mature novel. Fully in control of the narrative voice and style, Hinton gathers all her themes and concerns together in a novel that brings her central character to necessary and life-changing knowledge in a convincing and satisfying plot. The big gray horse Star Runner, a powerful (and dangerous) mythic presence, powerfully argues the need for discipline in one's personal and creative life. In the contest between rural and urban settings, the rural is clearly the victor, at least in terms of inspiring intellectual creativity.

## SOURCES FOR FURTHER STUDY

Campbell, Patty. Review of *Taming the Star Runner*, by S. E. Hinton. *The New York Times Book Review*, April 2, 1989, 26.

Daly, Jay. "*Taming the Star Runner*: Time Revisited." In *Presenting S. E. Hinton*. Boston: Twayne Publishers, 1989.

Mills, Randall K. "The Novels of S. E. Hinton: Springboard to Personal Growth for Adolescents." *Adolescence* 22 (Fall 1987): 641–646.

# Other Works

**RUMBLE FISH** (1975). In this bleak novel, brothers Rusty-James, age fourteen, and Motorcycle Boy, age seventeen, live with their educated but alcoholic father on welfare. Their mother ran off to California years earlier. The brothers fight members of rival gangs, steal aimlessly, go to school, and nurse wounds acquired in various fights. Motorcycle Boy, who has no friends, goes to California to look, unsuccessfully, for his mother. He suffers from intermittent psychologically caused deafness and color blindness. Despite his strangeness, people give Motorcycle Boy an odd kind of respect. Rusty-James is expelled from school, and his girlfriend, Patty, breaks up with him. He and his friend Steve are attacked by other hoods, and Motorcycle Boy appears to rescue them. When Steve gets home, his father gives him a serious beating.

Rusty-James is dethroned as the gang leader by Smoky. Motorcycle Boy breaks into a pet store, frees the animals, carries the Rumble Fish to the river, and is gunned down by the police. As Rusty-James is slammed up against the police car, he sees his brother die and sees also that he, like Motorcycle Boy, is now color-blind.

The novel is notable for Hinton's skillful use of imagery, metaphor, and mythology to reveal character by description and association. The images of color and its absence, of seeing and not seeing, of peace and violence, and of totemic animals (rabbit, panther, dog) identified with specific characters all give structure to and inform the book. Motorcycle Boy is a misfit on a flawed and fatal quest.

**THAT WAS THEN, THIS IS NOW** (1971). This novel is a story of orphans, of two friends, of the passage of time, of betrayal, and of the loss of innocence. Mark the "Lion" and Bryon,

Mickey Rourke (left) played the role of Motorcycle Boy and Matt Dillon, acting in his third movie adapted from a Hinton novel, played the part of Rusty-James in the 1983 motion picture *Rumble Fish*. Due to the intense Oklahoma heat in summer, most of the film was shot at night.

both sixteen, live together because Mark's parents killed each other in a fight that Mark witnessed. Bryon's father is also dead, and his mother is in the hospital. Mark, a thief, and Bryon, a hustler, hustle pool players in a local bar, hot-wire to "borrow" cars and occasionally, beat up hippies, and get into fights with the Shepard gang.

Bryon is sensitive to the economic divide that exists between the poor whites and the rich kids. He takes honors classes, where most of the students are the more well-off Socs, and he does not fit in. Bryon and Mark's friend Charlie is killed while saving Bryon and Mark from two tough ex-cons whom they had hustled at pool. Later, when Bryon falls in love with Cathy Carlson, the sister of M&M, a younger and very serious friend, Mark begins to realize that he and Cathy are competing for Bryon's friendship. Finally, when Mark begins dealing drugs to make

desperately needed money, his friendship with Bryon turns sour. As Mark sees it, life must be taken as it comes. He believes he cannot change the hand he has been dealt by life, but his fatalistic attitude and his refusal to examine the consequences of his actions do not serve him well.

Bryon and Cathy go in search of M&M, who has run away from his brutal father. They finally locate him taking refuge in a hippie flophouse in Tulsa and suffering from a bad acid trip. Bryon believes that Mark may have given the acid to M&M. In anger and in an attempt to score points with Cathy, he betrays Mark to the police. Deeply hurt by Bryon's betrayal, Mark refuses to defend himself and is sentenced to five years in the state reformatory. Their boyhood friendship is permanently ruptured. Bryon turns numb and—his innocence gone—wishes he were "a kid again, when [he] had all the answers."

A book written at the disciplined rate of two pages a day, *That Was Then, This Is Now* shows Hinton working effectively with myth and animal imagery. Bryon, the narrator, is established early on as a liar, and Hinton works with the narrative problem of an unreliable narrator. Perhaps this choice amplifies Bryon's turning in of Mark as more a betrayal than a laudable expression of social consciousness. In short, there are no heroes in the story, only the destructive and bleak consequences of wrong choices made in the absence of parents and a functioning family.

## Resources

No major collections of S. E. Hinton's work are held in libraries or archives. Sources of interest for readers of Hinton include the following:

**Official S. E. Hinton Web Site.** This site offers a biography, synopses of every Hinton book, and information on film adaptations of her works. Also featured is a page on frequently asked questions, which are addressed by Hinton herself. (http://www.sehinton.com)

**Boston Public Library Speech.** Hinton gave a talk at the Boston Public Library on September 20, 1980. An audio recording is available. (http://webpages.marshall.edu/~webb66/secondarybib.html)

**The Outsiders Home Page.** This site offers quizzes and work sheets on the novel, which students might find helpful to use as study guides. (http://www.forks.wednet.edu/middle/outsiderspage.html)

**Secondary Bibliography.** This site is a catalog of dozens of books, articles, and reviews on Hinton's works. Interviews and speeches are also listed. (http://webpages.marshall.edu/~webb66/secondarybib.html)

*THEODORE C. HUMPHREY*

# Index

Page numbers in **boldface** type indicate article titles.  Page numbers in *italic* type indicate illustrations.